99 World-Changing People
Influenced by the Bible

B

museum of the Bible

BOOKS

Executive Editorial Team
Allen Quine
Wayne Hastings
Jeana Ledbetter
Byron Williamson

Managing Editor
Christopher D. Hudson

Senior Editors
Jennifer Stair
Cynthia Tucker

Worthy Editorial
Kyle Olund
Leeanna Nelson

Design & Page Layout
Hudson Bible

Cover Design
Matt Smartt,
Smartt Guys design

99 World-Changing People Influenced by the Bible
© 2018 Museum of the Bible, Inc., Washington, DC 20014
Published by Worthy Publishing Group, a division of Worthy Media, Inc. in association with Museum of the Bible.

ISBN-10: 1945470356
ISBN-13: 978-1945470356

Cataloging-in-Publication Data is on file with the Library of Congress.

Produced with the assistance of Hudson Bible (www.HudsonBible.com).

Cover image: Tim Graham / Alamy Stock Photo

Printed in the USA

1 2 3 4 5 6 7 8 9 LBM 23 22 21 20 19 18

museum of the Bible
BOOKS

WORTHY®
PUBLISHING

Introduction 5

99 World-Changing People Influenced by the Bible

Introduction

The ***Guinness Book of World Records*** states that the Bible has sold more than 5 billion copies and has been translated into more than 2,200 languages. It has influenced our language tremendously and is quoted more often than other works of antiquity. It is no surprise, then, that several of our most prominent leaders have been influenced by the Bible.

Christian scholar Arthur Pink wrote, "The influence of the Bible is worldwide. Its mighty power has affected every department of human activity. The contents of the Scriptures have supplied themes for the greatest poets, artists, and musicians which the world has yet produced, and have been the mightiest factor of all in shaping the moral progress of the race."

From every walk of life, many of our leaders have read, quoted, and professed living by the tenets of the Bible. The Bible has been a source of comfort and guidance for everyone from poets, to musicians, to athletes, to scientists, to artists, to royalty, and even all the way up to the presidential office.

And while it has impacted and shaped well-known people, it continues to shape and impact people of all backgrounds and faiths.

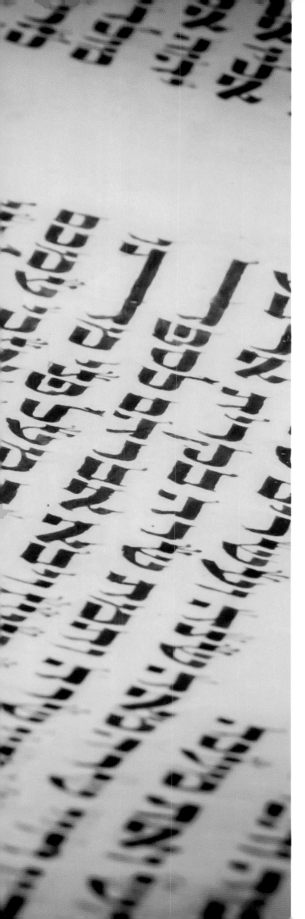

01

Rabbi Haninah Ben Teradion

Haninah was a teacher who oversaw a Torah academy in Sakhnin (in lower Galilee) during the second century. He was admired for his ability to teach and for how he handled charity funds honestly. Because he refused to follow the ban on teaching the Torah (the first five books of the Hebrew Bible), he was martyred. In fact, according to tradition, he was among the renowned rabbis that the Romans killed over a period of many years who were known as the Ten Martyrs. During Yom Kippur, the traditional Ashkenazic liturgy includes a poem called Eileh Ezkerah ("These do I recall"), which memorializes the ten brave rabbis.

There are different theories about how Rabbi Haninah died, but one legend states that Haninah was tried and then sentenced to death along with his wife. Just moments before Haninah was burned alive with a Torah scroll wrapped around him, he said, "If I alone would be burnt, the matter would be hard for me. [But] now, since I am burnt and the Torah scroll together with me, He who resents the insults offered to the Torah scroll will resent the insult offered to me." ■

Top: The Knesset Menorah, Jerusalem (detail - Haninah ben Teradion)
Left: Torah "yad" pointer and the ancient Hebrew text of the Book of Genesis in the Torah scroll.

02 Emperor Constantine

According to one account, Constantine was riding toward Rome to confront an enemy that had an army four times the size of his own when he saw a vision of a huge cross which contained the phrase "By this sign conquer" in the afternoon sky. The account also says that Jesus appeared to Constantine in a dream asking him to carry the cross into battle as his standard.

Constantine's contemporary biographer, Eusebius, the Bishop of Caesarea in Palestine, reported that Constantine was awe-struck by the vision and decided to devote himself from then on to the reading of the Scriptures. To assist him in his studies, he selected priests to be his advisers and sought to learn more about Christian doctrine.

According to Eusebius, Constantine began making substantial donations to the church and to the poor.

Historians have debated for centuries what exactly motivated Flavius Valerius Constantinus, who would become Roman emperor Constantine I, to profess Christianity. However, what is not debated is that the emperor was responsible for a turning point in world history: he extended freedom of worship to all within the Roman Empire, including Christians.

Born in what is now Serbia, Constantine was the son of a deputy emperor of the Roman Empire. He spent time in the Eastern imperial court, and later accompanied his father on military campaigns. When his father died, he was thrust into a fierce political battle for control of the empire. Constantine invaded Italy and won a key battle at the Milvian Bridge near Rome against his rival, Maxentius. After this victory, Constantine became the emperor of the Western empire in 312. After further victories against other rivals, he became emperor of the entire Roman empire in 324.

Constantine waited until he was near death to be baptized as a Christian himself. This was not an unusual practice, and Constantine reportedly felt it was time to be purified of the sins from his life as an emperor.

During his reign, Constantine played an important role in overseeing the early church's most important council, the Council of Nicaea in 325, to settle controversies that threatened the unity of the church. The resulting Nicene Creed became a standard for Christian orthodoxy. Nicaea was called to deal with Arianism and the matter of Easter. ∎

Top: Bronze statue of Constantine I in York, England, near the spot where he was proclaimed Augustus in 306
Left: Arch of Constantine, Rome. The Arch was built in 315 AD to celebrate emperor Constantine's victory in 312 over emperor Maxentius.

03

Saint Augustine

Saint Augustine changed the shape of Christianity largely through his books *Confessions* and *The City of God*. They are still read and considered relevant today.

The son of a pagan father and a Christian mother who was born in what is now Algeria, Augustine committed himself to the study of rhetoric. Later, he reflected on his youth. In *Confessions*, he writes that his very nature was flawed. "It was foul, and I loved it. I loved my own error—not that for which I erred, but the error itself."

It was during this tumultuous time that Augustine prayed his famous prayer: "Grant me chastity and continence, but not yet."

As a student of rhetoric, Augustine enjoyed listening to priests' homilies. He was affected deeply by the teaching of Saint Ambrose, the bishop of Milan, and slowly began to change his lifestyle. After his mother died, Augustine gave the proceeds from the sale of his property to the poor, returned to Africa, and founded a monastery. He was appointed a presbyter in 391 and then a bishop around 396.

Augustine was a significant influence on theology and philosophy, adapting ancient Greek Platonic philosophy to Christian and Roman ideas. He was influential in developing the idea of sacred and secular realms—one where the rule of God reigns supreme, and the other where the rule of man does. One was destined for eternal salvation, the other for eternal damnation. With this theme, Augustine developed the belief in hell as a place of eternal torment for unrepentant sinners.

The subject of free will versus predestination was controversial during Augustine's time. He asserted that original sin makes internal renewal and moral behavior impossible for humans if it were not for the accidental and undeserved grace of God.

A lifelong student of the Bible, Augustine examined its words and phrases closely. For example, in his *Confessions*, he explored the different meanings of "In the beginning," which opens the Book of Genesis. He theorized that the phrase can be taken literally (as in the beginning of time) or that "in the Beginning" meant "in

S. AGUSTIN.

the eternal Word" or "in Divine Wisdom," the heavens and the earth were created. As a part of this discussion, Augustine contemplated the meaning of the "past" and "present" and the meanings of "heaven" and "earth."

Augustine believed that it was up to the Holy Spirit to reveal the true meaning of the Bible to readers. In his closing to *Confessions*, he refers directly to the words of Jesus in Matthew 7:7-12 ("Ask, and it shall be given you; seek, and ye shall find; knock, and it shall be opened unto you") with this passage:

"What man will give another man the understanding of this, or what angel will give another angel, or what angel will give a man? Of You we must ask, in You we must seek, at You we must knock. Thus only shall we receive, thus shall we find, thus will it be opened to us."

When the Vandals invaded North Africa, they set siege to Hippo, a fortified city. Three months into the siege, Augustine, age seventy-six, died from a fever. Amazingly, his many writings survived the Vandal takeover, and his theology has influenced the church ever since. ■

Top: St. Augustine, Colored engraving

04 Saint Patrick

Every March 17, people drink green beer, hang shamrocks as decorations, and wear shirts proclaiming, "Kiss me; I'm Irish." Have you ever wondered what all the fuss is about?

Saint Patrick's Day honors the patron saint of Ireland. Although he was never canonized, and he wasn't even Irish, Patrick is largely responsible for converting Ireland to Christianity in the fifth century.

Born in Britain, Patrick (whose given name is believed to be Maewyn Succat) was abducted by Irish raiders when he was sixteen. His father was a deacon in the church, and Patrick wrote in his autobiography, *Confessio*, that his faith helped sustain him through six years of slavery in Ireland.

Eventually, he was able to escape and make it back to his family in Britain. However, he had a dream in which he was called to spread the gospel to Ireland. Patrick studied to be a priest and was ordained as a bishop. When he was in his forties, he returned to Ireland to spread the gospel according to his vision.

Patrick was familiar with the Irish clan system from his years as a slave. He frequently used two of the Ten Commandments to support his missionary work, as described in his letter to soldiers who had killed Irish Christians: "You shall not murder" (Exodus 20:13) and "You shall not covet . . . anything that belongs to your neighbor" (Exodus 20:17).

Patrick became a legendary figure. You may have heard that he drove the snakes out of Ireland into the sea to their destruction. This story is unlikely to be based on truth. Another legend claims Patrick used the shamrock—a three-leaved plant with one stem—to explain the Holy Trinity to farmers and herders. Traditionally, the Irish—and those who want to be Irish for a day—wear a shamrock, the national plant of Ireland, on Saint Patrick's Day. ■

Top: St. Patrick in an early 19th century print showing him trampling a serpent
Left: St. Patrick's hat with four-leaf clover

05 Pope Gregory the Great

Sometimes called the founder of the medieval papacy, Pope Gregory the Great led the post-Roman Empire church through a chaotic time of war, disease, and invasions.

Gregory was born into a wealthy aristocratic Roman family with a house on the city's prestigious Caelian Hill. He had established a successful career as a prefect, an administrative officer in Rome. However in his thirties, Gregory decided to give away his money, turn the family home into a monastery, and become a monk.

He went on to found other monasteries and eventually was called to serve Pope Pelagius II as a deacon. Gregory was elected as the pope when Pelagius died in 590.

Gregory also performed imperial tasks, frequently stepping in to negotiate with barbarian invaders to keep them from invading Rome and thereby protecting citizens from harm and loss of property.

Gregory is also traditionally credited with an important contribution to Western music, the tradition of plainsong, a simple melody sung a cappella. This singing of the Psalms developed into the chants that still bear Gregory's name. Gregorian chants are monophonic lines of verse that are often sung during the various parts of Mass.

Gregory's surviving works include homilies, lectures, and commentaries on biblical books. He often employed medieval methods of biblical interpretation. He also implemented reform in the Western liturgy.

A humble man, Gregory called himself "a servant of the servants of God." Lamed by arthritis near the end of his life, Gregory was buried in the basilica of Saint Peter. He was canonized soon after his death in 604. ∎

Top: Pope Gregory the Great, portrait
Left: St. Peter's Basilica in Rome, Italy

06 Charlemagne

Charlemagne, who was also known as Charles the Great, is sometimes called the father of Europe.

By the time of his death, the medieval leader ruled over an empire that extended from modern France in the west to modern Poland in the east.

Charlemagne became ruler of all the Frankish realms in 771. He then rose to become the first Holy Roman Emperor, consecrated by Pope Leo III in Rome on Christmas Day in 800. His empire included people of many different languages and customs, but the moral and doctrinal teachings of Christianity were central to his purpose as a leader. In fact, his kingdom was defined not as much by geography as by its religious unity. His kingdom became known as Christendom.

Charlemagne spent much of his reign engaged in sweeping military campaigns. His troops conquered the Lombards from present-day northern Italy and the Avars from modern-day Austria, Hungary, and Bavaria. He also earned a reputation for extreme ruthlessness, waging a thirty-year-long war against the Saxons, a Germanic pagan tribe.

The reigns of Charlemagne and his immediate successors became known as the Carolingian Renaissance, a name taken from "Carol," an old French word for "Charles." This period of cultural renewal was inspired in part by Charlemagne's desire to teach Christians the Bible and how to perform church liturgy correctly.

The period spurred an increase in literacy, the creation of new forms of writing, the development of a royal library for scholarly research, and the emergence of new forms of literature, all of which had a profound effect on European culture.

Charlemagne was influenced by Augustine's book, *The City of God*, and he believed the church and state should work as one to unify society. He also demonstrated that, like Constantine, he believed he was the overlord of the church.

As king, Charlemagne read the Bible but was disturbed by the discrepancies and unreliable linguistics of the handwritten texts in his possession. He was determined to produce a more consistent Latin text of the Bible, so he enlisted scholar Alcuin of York to create a more correct biblical text. Charlemagne then presented

this updated version of the Latin Vulgate Bible to the people of his kingdom.

In a letter to Pope Leo III, Charlemagne wrote, "Our task is externally, with God's help, to defend with our arms the holy Church of Christ against attacks by the heathen from any side and against devastation by the infidels and, internally, to strengthen the Church by the recognition of the Catholic faith. Your share, Most Holy Father, is to support our army with hands upraised to God, as did Moses in ancient days, so that the . . . name of our Lord Jesus Christ may be glorified throughout the world." ∎

Top: Charlemagne, aka Charles the Great or Charles I. 18th century engraving.

07 Pope Innocent III

As one the of the most powerful of the medieval popes, Pope Innocent III expanded the papal authority; launched multiple crusades to Spain, southern France, and Jerusalem; and helped to reform many practices within the church.

Born in Italy as Lothar of Segni, Innocent reigned as pope from 1198 to 1216 at the height of medieval Catholicism. He was able to cement his authority over the Papal States, territories that were designed to protect him and his office against foreign invasion.

Innocent sent crusaders to conquer Jerusalem, and pitted the force of his office against what he perceived as heretical movements in Italy and Southern France. In his pursuit of papal authority, he went head-to-head with European monarchs.

For instance, when King John of England would not accept Stephen Langton's appointment as archbishop of Canterbury, Innocent excommunicated him and invited King Philip Augustus of France to invade England. He also declared the Magna Carta null and void because King John had signed it without his consent.

Innocent quoted Jeremiah 1:10 to describe his own view of his papal power. He would have said it in Latin, but translated into the King James Version, it reads: "I have this day set thee over the nations and over the kingdoms, to root out, and to pull down, and to destroy, and to throw down, to build, and to plant."

Pope Innocent III presided over the Fourth Lateran Council in 1215, which reformed many church practices. For example, the Council forbade priests from participating in the procedure in which defendants would be forced to scald themselves or otherwise injure themselves in an attempt for the court to determine guilt or innocence. ▪

Top: Pope Innocent III. From The National and Domestic History of England by William Aubrey published circa 1890.
Left: Crusader in armor

08 Saint Francis of Assisi

Have you ever seen a bird feeder or birdbath made in the image of Saint Francis of Assisi? Legend has it that Saint Francis had a special relationship with birds.

According to one story, birds landed on his outstretched arms and listened quietly at his feet while he gave a sermon. Another legend relates that Francis was able to quiet a large flock of noisy birds that were interrupting a religious service.

Only two years after his death, Francis was honored as a saint. He had a reputation as someone who was kind and gentle, committed to his faith and to serving others. Yet Francis once had quite a different reputation.

Born Giovanni di Bernardone, the son of a wealthy Italian cloth merchant, he was a cavalier, worldly young man. Francis's carefree days ended in 1202, however, when he fought as a soldier to defend Assisi from troops from the town of Perugia.

He spent a year as a prisoner of war. After experiencing discontent with his former way of life, in 1208, he believed he had a calling to sell his possessions and preach to people.

Inspired by the teachings of the Bible, Francis established the Franciscans, a religious order centered on self-sacrifice, preaching the Christian message of salvation, and helping those in need. His original band of twelve followers grew and ignited a religious revival that spread across Europe.

Today, the Franciscans are still active internationally. The Franciscan Friars of the United States, for instance, has more than 1,000 members of the Order of Friars Minor ministering as brothers across the country. ∎

Top: St. Francis of Assisi preaching to the birds
Down: Panorama of Assisi (Italy) with Saint Francis Cathedral

09 Thomas Aquinas

Sometimes called "the dumb ox" by his peers because of his girth and because one of his eyes was noticeably larger than the other, Thomas Aquinas was a quiet, introspective young man.

Aquinas's parents desired him to be a Benedictine monk, and were so upset when he joined the Dominican Order at the age of nineteen that they kidnapped him and likely forced him to remain at their home—the castle of Monte San Giovanni Campano in Roccasecca, Italy.

However, when his mother saw her son's determination to observe the rules of the monastic order even when he was home, she changed her mind.

Aquinas went on to become one of the most influential thinkers of the Middle Ages. By combining the concepts of faith and reason—previously thought to be separate and distinct—he became important to the studies of theology and philosophy.

Aquinas was influenced by the Bible, Christian theology, Aristotle, and other classical thinkers. In his five-volume systematic theology, *Summa Theologica*, considered to be his most important and enduring work, Aquinas asserted that revelation guides reason and that reason clarifies faith. Using his knowledge of the Bible to support his points, Aquinas argued that combining faith and reason can prove the existence of God.

Aquinas also taught that, while people can learn some things about God (such as the Trinity) from the Bible, one can know other information (such as the complexity of the human body) by studying God's revelation in nature. He also taught that one can know

some things through both special revelation and natural revelation. His example of this combination is the knowledge that God exists.

According to Aquinas's teachings, all truth is God's truth and therefore universal and permanent.

Today, the writings of Thomas Aquinas continue to influence modern thought, with people as varied as neuroscientist and philosopher Walter Freeman III and the famous Irish writer James Joyce acknowledging his influence on their work. ∎

Top: Thomas Aquinas, 1476, artist unknown
Left: Germany--c. 1974: A stamp printed in Germany issued for the 700th anniversary of the death of St. Thomas Aquinas shows St. Thomas teaching pupils

10 Dante

The epitaph of Dante Alighieri, known to the world simply as Dante, begins, "Dante the theologian, skilled in every branch of knowledge that philosophy may cherish in her illustrious bosom."

Dante was indeed a man skilled in many fields of study. Known primarily as the writer of the epic poem *The Divine Comedy*, Dante was also a theologian, philosopher, and political thinker who influenced modern Western literature and modern conceptions of heaven and hell.

T. S. Eliot is one of the major poets of the twentieth century, and he once compared Dante with Shakespeare, explaining that they "divide the modern world between them. There is no third."

Born in Florence to a family of low aristocracy, Dante was captivated by a girl named Beatrice Portinari while he was a boy. Although the two may never have even exchanged words, his feelings for Beatrice dominated his life and his work.

Using vivid imagery, Dante combines the classical heritage of Greece and Rome with biblical accounts. In *The Divine Comedy*, which describes Dante's journey through hell, purgatory, and heaven, we learn what happens when the love of earthly things (Beatrice) is confused with the love of God. Dante placed numerous biblical characters, classical heroes and villains, and famous church officials in the various levels of the afterlife.

In Dante's *Inferno*, we travel with the poet through the nine circles of hell, along with his guide. Dante's depiction of hell draws from the biblical accounts from the book of Revelation. He describes a sealed abyss in which Satan dwells (Revelation 20:3) and the sinful dead being thrown into a lake of fire (Revelation 20:14). He also draws on other sources, including Virgil's *Aeneid*.

Dante finished *The Divine Comedy* not long before his death, and it was quickly recognized by his contemporaries. By the year 1400, scholars had written at least twelve commentaries on the poem's meaning and significance. It continues to be studied as part of the Western literary canon today. ∎

Top: Florence Duomo. Basilica di Santa Maria del Fiore Basilica of Saint Mary of the Flower in Florence, Italy.
Right: Dante statue located in Piazza Santa Croce, Florence, Italy.

11 John Wycliffe

Not many people can rile things up several decades after their death, but that is exactly what John Wycliffe did. Forty-three years after his death, his body was exhumed, his remains were burned, and his ashes were dumped into the river.

Nevertheless, Wycliffe's influence continues to this day. As one 17th-century church historian put it: "The ashes of Wycliffe are the emblem of his doctrine which now is dispersed the world over." Wycliffe is called "the morning star of the Reformation."

Part theologian, part philosopher, and part preacher, Wycliffe believed that the Bible had greater authority than the pope. He also believed the Bible should be taught and read in the vernacular language. After his death, Wycliffe's followers finished the first complete English translation of the Bible.

Church officials considered Wycliffe's translations a challenge to their power and influence, and they accused him of blasphemy. They were concerned about heresy and the proper interpretation of the Bible in the hands of laypeople. A contemporary commentator contended, "By this translation, the Scriptures have become vulgar, and they are more available to lay, and even to women who can read, than they were to learned scholars, who have a high intelligence. So, the pearl of the gospel is scattered and trodden underfoot by swine."

Wycliffe, however, had written, "Englishmen learn Christ's law best in English. Moses heard God's law in his own tongue; so did Christ's apostles."

In his teachings, Wycliffe also challenged the church on other points of doctrine, exhorting his listeners to "Trust wholly in Christ; rely altogether on his sufferings; beware of seeking to be justified in any other way than by his righteousness." Although a council of theologians later decreed that his writings were heretical and the government condemned his teachings, Wycliffe died before he could be punished for his alleged crimes. ∎

Top: John Wycliffe translating the Bible into English

12 Johannes Gutenberg

When he invented metal movable type and a new printing press, Johannes Gutenberg transformed the world.

At a time when books and other information had to be laboriously written out by hand or produced by inefficient types of block printing, the printing press made the mass production of printed materials possible. The invention led to a wider dissemination of knowledge and a more literate society than ever before.

Born in Mainz, Germany, Johannes Gutenberg likely worked as a blacksmith and a goldsmith. In 1436, he developed an idea for movable type and began combining some existing technology for wooden block printing that pressed ink onto paper. His metallic components representing letters and punctuation marks could be moved and reconfigured to print different pages of text.

After about ten years of working on a prototype, his invention could print much faster than the previous block method.

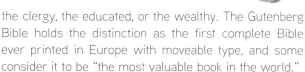

The first major book Gutenberg produced with his printing press was the forty-two line Bible, a version of the Latin Vulgate that that became known as the Gutenberg Bible. Prior to its publication, Bibles were handwritten, and, as a result, they were in short supply and usually unavailable to anyone outside the clergy, the educated, or the wealthy. The Gutenberg Bible holds the distinction as the first complete Bible ever printed in Europe with moveable type, and some consider it to be "the most valuable book in the world."

Gutenberg only printed 180 copies of the Gutenberg Bible, and went bankrupt. But he paved the way for Bible literacy among laypeople. Soon thousands of other books were printed on Gutenberg's printing press.

Gutenberg's innovation transformed the world in much the same way the Internet has in modern times. Knowledge became more readily available, allowing people to read and spread ideas faster and farther than ever before. ∎

Top: Replica of printing press by Gutenberg
Left: Old engraved illustration of Johannes Gensfleisch zur Laden zum Gutenberg bronze statue by David Hazard. June 24, 1840 in Strasbourg, France.

13 Christopher Columbus

Years ago, American schoolchildren memorized the phrase, "In fourteen hundred ninety-two Columbus sailed the ocean blue" to help them recall the year Christopher Columbus sailed into the Americas (specifically present-day Haiti and the Dominican Republic).

In recent decades, however, Columbus the man and Columbus the explorer have faced intense scrutiny. Whether you believe Columbus was a hero worth celebrating or a villain worth scorning, you may not know that he believed that his famous voyage fulfilled an ancient prophecy from the Bible.

"God made me the messenger of the new heaven and the new earth of which he spoke in the Apocalypse of Saint John after having spoken of it through the mouth of Isaiah," wrote Columbus in a letter, circa 1500. "And he showed me the spot where to find it."

After more than thirty days of sailing, Columbus arrived in what became known as the "New World" on October 12, 1492. In his journal, Columbus indicated that he was influenced by the Bible (Zechariah 9:10) to carry the Christian gospel to the end of the world. He also found assurance in Psalm 107:23–24, which says, "Some went down to the sea in ships, doing business on great waters; they saw the deeds of the LORD, his wondrous works in the deep."

In 1493, Columbus went back across the ocean with 1,200 men, including priests and farmers, to establish a colony and to plant Christianity in the new land. ∎

Right: Statue of Christopher Columbus, Barcelona, Spain.

14 Leonardo da Vinci

When you think of a Renaissance man, it is hard not to consider Leonardo da Vinci. Scientist, artist, inventor—he did it all.

A true genius, Leonardo drew plans for such diverse inventions as the multibarreled gun (a forerunner of the modern machine gun), armored car, bicycle, parachute, helicopter, and airplane. He also made the first accurate drawings of human anatomy.

Born near Florence, Italy, Leonardo demonstrated great talent at an early age. He kept detailed notebooks with his thoughts, ideas, and plans, including some 2,500 drawings. Although many of his amazing ideas never came to fruition (at least during his lifetime), he is well known for several of his paintings: the *Mona Lisa,* his portrait of a woman with a mysterious smile, *The Adoration of the Magi,* and the largest, *The Last Supper.*

Ludovico Sforza, duke of Milan, commissioned the twenty-nine-by-fifteen-foot painting, and Leonardo spent nearly eighteen years working on it. This painting of the Passover meal captures the moment after Jesus reveals that one of his disciples will betray him. The artist paid special attention to detail, placing John ("the one whom Jesus loved,"

according to John 20:2) to the right of Jesus and showing the distinct emotions of each of the twelve men.

Leonardo experimented with a mixture of oil and tempera paint in order to capture the look of an oil painting on a wall. The idea worked. However, even during the master's lifetime, the paint began to deteriorate. More damage occurred in the seventeenth century, when, unbelievably, someone cut a door into the bottom of the painting. In addition, the painting came close to being destroyed by a bomb during World War II.

The Last Supper has been restored several times over the centuries. In April 2017, Eataly, an Italian marketplace, announced that it would sponsor an initiative to preserve *The Last Supper.* The company plans to install an air-filtration system to prevent further damage due to atmospheric pollution that causes the painted surfaces to crumble away. The filtration system is scheduled to be operational by 2019 to mark the 500th anniversary of da Vinci's death. ∎

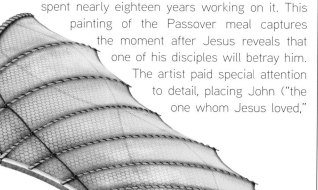

Top: Leonardo da Vinci, engraving by Cosomo Colombini, ca. 1500.
Left: The classic Leonardo Da Vinci flying machine, otherwise known as an ornithopter.

Leonardo da Vinci (1452 - 1519) "Mona Lisa" La Gioconda. Reproduction from illustrated Encyclopedia "Treasures of Art," Russia , 1906 **21**

15 Nicolaus Copernicus

As part of his training to become a church official, Polish born Nicolaus Copernicus studied the stars. At the time, it was thought that a solid background in reading the heavens—in the hope of anticipating future events—could benefit both clergy and doctors.

While a student at the University of Bologna in 1496, Copernicus worked with astronomer Domenico Maria de Novara, helping him with his research and recording observations of the heavens. The accepted belief then was that the earth was the center of the universe.

When he returned home to Poland in 1503, he resumed his position as Canon of Frauenburg Cathedral and continued his studies of the night sky on his own. Copernicus established a reputation as an astronomer. In fact, it is believed that Copernicus was among the experts consulted by Pope Leo X in 1514 when the church was revising its calendar.

What Copernicus discovered would revolutionize not only astronomy but also the way humans thought about their place in the cosmos. In 1543, he published *De Revolutionibus Orbium Coelestium* (On the Revolutions of the Celestial Spheres), in which he explained his

controversial theory that the earth rotates daily on its axis and circles the sun yearly. Copernicus's findings challenged the prevailing and incorrect model of the solar system which had held sway for 1,400 years, since the days of Ptolemy of Alexandria.

His theories became the foundation for the work of other astronomers, including Galileo, who, a century later, was placed under house arrest as a heretic for promoting that the earth orbited the sun.

Copernicus did not view his theories as a violation of the Bible or as a challenge to the church. He even wrote in the preface to *De Revolutionibus*, addressed to the pope, "If perchance there shall be idle talkers, who, though they are ignorant of all mathematical sciences, nevertheless assume the right to pass judgment on these things, and if they should dare to criticise and attack this theory of mine because of some passage of Scripture which they have falsely distorted for their own purpose, I care not at all; I will even despise their judgment as foolish." ∎

Top: Torun Monument of Nicolaus Copernicus
Left: Triquetrum, instrument for astrometry used by Nicolaus Copernicus to determine positions of stars and other objects in sky

16 Bartolomé de las Casas

Bartolomé de las Casas was a priest, who controlled an estate on the island of Hispaniola, in the New World, that used slave labor. He was one of the first people to speak out against the oppression and slavery of the native population of the New World. How did a slave owner become an outspoken advocate for human rights?

Like many of his contemporaries, las Casas, who was the son of a merchant, looked to the Americas as a source of wealth and power. For his efforts in various Spanish missions, he was awarded land on the island of Hispaniola, which Christopher Columbus claimed for Spain in 1492. Along with his new property, las Casas assumed authority over the native people living there.

At first, las Casas worked as a public official and soldier and in 1512, became the first Catholic priest to be ordained in the New World in 1513. Later writing that "all the world is human!'" Las Casas gave up his land and freed his slaves and traveled to Spain to attempt to convince authorities to end the cruel treatment of the native peoples.

In denouncing the Spanish exploitation of the native peoples, las Casas cited Romans 10 and Hebrews 2 from the Bible as support of the native people's human rights. Las Casas was particularly moved by a passage found

in the Catholic Bible's Sirach 34:21–22: "The bread of the needy is the life of the poor; who deprives them of it is a man of blood. To take away a neighbor's living is to murder him; to deprive a laborer of his wages is to shed blood."

Las Casas was met with strong resistance, but he continued to preach, write, and petition the king about protection for the Native Americans.

His major work, *A Short Account of the Destruction of the Indie*, was written as an effort to persuade the Spanish royalty and nation to end slavery and other practices that the Spanish were using against the indigenous populations of the New World. At the same time, other figures, such as Juan Ginés de Sepúlveda (1489-1573), were referring to the Bible in their arguments for the continuation of slavery.

Simón Bolívar, the nineteenth-century Venezuelan revolutionary, was inspired by las Casas's letters and writings in his struggle against Spain, as were the leaders of the movement for Mexican independence from Spain. ■

Top: Friar Bartolome de las Casas. General Archive of the Indies. Seville, Spain
Left: Old engravings depicted Bartolomé de las Casas

17 Henry VIII of England

Best known for his tumultuous six marriages and perhaps also for images of him as a large man with a big appetite, Henry VIII of England declared himself head of the Church of England in 1534, separating the English church from papal control.

After the death of his older brother Arthur in 1502, Henry became heir to the throne of his father, Henry VII. He obtained permission from the pope to marry his brother's widow, Catherine of Aragon.

At six feet in height—extremely tall at the time—the eighteen-year-old prince was considered athletic and charming when he took the crown in 1509. To assure the continuation of the new Tudor dynasty, Henry was eager to have a male heir. When Catherine produced no male children, Henry wanted to end the marriage, and he appealed to the pope for an annulment.

When the pope refused, Henry retaliated by declaring England separate from the church and by appointing himself as the supreme governor of the Church of England. He divorced Catherine and married Anne Boleyn. When Anne also failed to have a son, the king had her beheaded on what historians assume were trumped-up charges of adultery and conspiracy.

Ironically, Pope Leo X gave Henry VIII the title of "Defender of the Faith" in 1521 as a reward for his "Declaration of the Seven Sacraments Against Martin Luther." When Henry broke with the church, Pope Paul III recanted the title, but Parliament officially bestowed it upon the monarch in 1544. It has been used by all successors to the English throne.

In Henry's final address to Parliament in 1545, he challenged Parliament and the clergy to put aside their differences and live up to the standards of Scripture, particularly Paul's instructions on "charity" (love) in 1 Corinthians 13. He noted, "I am very sorry to know and hear how unreverently that most precious jewel, the word of God, is disputed, rhymed, sung, and jangled in every alehouse and tavern, contrary to the true meaning and doctrine of the same."

Henry's decision to separate England from the Roman Catholic Church had far-reaching implications. It led to a series of religious conflicts, some of which caused the development of religious sects that eventually founded new colonies in America. ∎

Top: Hampton Court Palace home of Henry VIII
Top-right: Henry VIII. Portrait by Hans Holbein the Younger (1497-1543). Oil on panel, 1540

18 Jacques Cartier

French explorer Jacques Cartier, the first Westerner to explore Canada, also gave the country its name. He chose the word Canada—from the Huron-Iroquois kanata, which means a village or settlement—to describe the area around what is now Quebec City, but the name stuck for the entire country.

Born in Saint-Malo, Brittany, France, Jacques Cartier became a respectable mariner and sailed to the Americas, where he proved himself to be a skilled explorer. Charged by France's King Francis I to find gold and other riches and to find a new route to Asia, Cartier led three voyages to the New World. His exploration of the Saint Lawrence River enabled France to lay claim to a large area of what would become Canada.

Initially, Cartier was disappointed by the Canadian coastline. The explorer drew on his knowledge of the Bible to reference the account of God's curse on Cain for the murder of his brother Abel when he wrote, "I am rather inclined to believe that this is the land God gave to Cain."

The explorer is also credited with founding the city of Montréal in 1533. He wrote in his diary, "We all kneeled down in the company of the Indians and with our hands raised toward heaven yielded our thanks to God."

Like other sixteenth-century explorers, Cartier and his men brought the Bible to the New World, and they shared biblical stories with Native Americans in hopes of converting them to Christianity. Cartier read the Gospel of John to Iroquois in 1535 and shared with them his concern for their well-being. ∎

Top: Jacques Cartier. Portrait. Color
Bottom: Jacques-Cartier Bridge in Montreal

19 William Tyndale

"My brother's keeper"
"The salt of the earth"
"Fight the good fight."
"The powers that be"
"The Lord bless thee, and keep thee. The Lord make his face shine upon thee."
"Thou shalt love the Lord thy God with all thine heart, with all thy soul, and with all thy might."

We owe these and many other well-known English phrases to William Tyndale.

Tyndale was the first person to translate the New Testament into English, working from Erasmus's edition of the Greek text. This historical feat not only introduced the Bible to many English-speaking readers throughout the western world, but it also helped establish some of the modern English language.

A priest and a scholar who supposedly could speak seven languages, William Tyndale had a passion for bringing the Bible to all people. In 1523, he requested permission from Cuthbert Tunstall, the bishop of London, to translate the New Testament into the English language, but he was denied.

After encountering further rejection in England for his project, Tyndale traveled throughout Europe and eventually went to the German city of Worms. There, he was able to produce 6,000 copies of the first English New Testament that he had translated from the Greek.

Historians tell us that when Tyndale smuggled his translated New Testaments back to England for distribution, it infuriated local bishops, who attempted to seize or buy up and destroy all the copies. The hunt was on for Tyndale, who was labeled a heretic. Tyndale was not deterred, however, as the sales actually financed his further work. While hiding in the city of Antwerp, he revised his New Testament translation and began translating the Old Testament (the Hebrew Bible).

Eventually, Tyndale was betrayed by someone posing as his friend. After being held in prison for more than a year, Tyndale was charged with heresy and condemned to death. In 1536, he was strangled and his body burned at the stake.

Although he died a martyr's death, Tyndale's work lives on today. When King James commissioned a new Bible translation in 1604, his writers relied on Tyndale's work, in addition to the Geneva and Bishop's Bibles. A 2015 study by Jon Nielson and Royal Skousen of Brigham Young University found that about 76% of the King James Version's Old Testament text and 84% of its New Testament text comes directly from Tyndale's translations. ∎

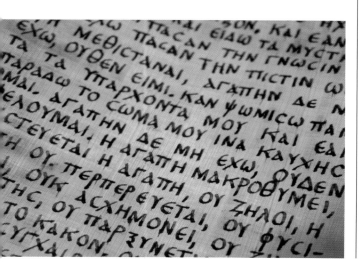

Top: William Tyndale, From Impressions of English Literature, published 1944.
Left: Greek Manuscript of 1st Corinthians 13 on Papyrus

20 John Calvin

Martin Luther sparked the beginnings of the Protestant Reformation when he wrote his ninety-five theses, and according to tradition, nailed them to the church door at Wittenberg. John Calvin was a significant second-generation leader in the Protestant Reformation, when he assisted the church in embracing the new reforms at Geneva. Whereas Luther brought passion to his cause, Calvin brought more of a quiet, intellectual approach.

Born in Noyon, France, John Calvin attended school in Paris, Orléans, and Bourges, which were intended to prepare him to study theology and to serve the church. However, in 1528, he ended his theological studies and began to study law. A few years later, he had what he described as a "sudden conversion," which caused him to increase his zeal to study what he called "true religion."

It was around this time that Calvin became fervent about Protestant teachings. Calvin attempted to standardize his understanding of Protestant theology and the Christian faith in his work, *Institutes of the Christian Religion*. He taught his followers about the sovereignty of God, the vital importance of Bible to sound doctrine, and about the concept of divine predestination—the doctrine that God chooses some to enter heaven based upon his power and grace. In the Institutes, Calvin presented the Bible as the way to see the "true God: "When aided by glasses, [one can] begin to read distinctly, so Scripture, gathering together the impressions of Deity, which, till then, lay confused in our minds, dissipates the darkness, and shows us the true God clearly."

In 1536, Calvin was traveling to Strasbourg and had to make an unexpected detour through Geneva, a city which had just voted to adopt the reformation a few months before. He was encouraged to stay and help with the reform of the church. After some controversy with the leaders there, he left for a time. But he soon returned and spent the remainder of his life there.

Geneva became a Protestant haven to refugees and exiles and a center of Protestant printing and scholarship. Calvin revised several editions of the French Bible.

Calvin left behind a legacy of sermons and commentaries on the Bible, and scholars acknowledge that his interpretation of Christianity had an influence on the development of political thought. For example, unlike many of his contemporaries, Calvin believed that it was the responsibility of the state not only to maintain order but also to promote the general welfare of a society. ∎

21 John Knox

A study of John Knox is a study of contrasts: Knox was a Christian minister who has been described as one of the most fiery and eloquent speakers of his day, yet only two of his sermons were published. He is considered the father of the Scottish Reformation, but today a parking lot covers his grave.

Born in a small town near Edinburgh, Scotland, John Knox studied theology at the University of Saint Andrews. Not much is known about his early life, but we do know he was ordained as a priest and then became a notary and a tutor to the sons of local Scottish nobility.

During this time, many Scots were angry with the Roman Catholic Church, which owned more than half of the Scottish land, and with church officials, many of whom were political appointees who led immoral lives. Influenced by John Calvin and English Protestants, Knox challenged the authority of the monarchy and believed that the Bible should be available to the common people.

In 1547, Knox was captured as a slave by French forces and forced to row in ships' galleys for nineteen months, in part because of his views about the Bible's role in public and private affairs.

He worked with Bible scholars to produce the Geneva Bible, a historically important English Bible translation that preceded the King James Version by sixty-one years.

Knox went on to coauthor the Scots Confession of Faith, a collection of twenty-five articles that served as the foundation for the Church of Scotland's doctrine until the Westminster Confession replaced it in 1647. He became a leading force in the establishment of the Presbyterian form of Calvinism in Scotland. ∎

Top: John Knox
Bottom: Reformation wall in Geneva

22 Teresa of Avila

In some ways, the biography of Saint Teresa of Avila, who was born Teresa de Cepeda y Ahumada, reads like that of a young girl.

She enjoyed fashion and popular fiction about knights and castles, and she liked to socialize with her friends. However, that is only part of her story.

Saint Teresa was born in Ávila, in the Crown of Castile (present-day Spain) to a wealthy family. She was close with her pious mother, and she helped her distribute alms to the poor and the needy. As a young girl, Teresa was kindhearted and prayed for long hours in silence.

When her mother died, fourteen-year-old Teresa sought solace in her faith. However, without her mother's daily influence, she became more interested in social activities. When she was sixteen, her father sent her to the Augustinian nuns at Ávila for her education. However, at the convent, Teresa became seriously ill and was forced to return home. After she recovered, she left home again, this time without her father's consent, to become a nun of the Carmelite Order and to lead a spiritual life.

Despite a lifetime of poor health, she wrote extensively about God, the Bible, and about Christianity, including the *Life of Saint Teresa of Jesus*, the *Book of the Foundations*, *The Way of Perfection*, *Spiritual Relations*, *Exclamations of the Soul to God*, *The Interior Castle*, and *Conceptions on the Love of God*.

In her books and other writings, Teresa analyzes the mystical experiences and visions she experienced, and emphasized an inner relationship with Jesus Christ, influencing generations of Christians and authors. Teresa is the founder of a religious order, the Discalced Carmelites, and was a reformer of the Carmelite order as part of the Catholic Reformation.

Canonized in 1622, Saint Teresa is the patron saint for headache sufferers. In 1970, she was declared a Doctor of the Church for her writings and teaching on prayer, one of only two women to receive that honor. ■

Top: Saint Teresa: Painting at the Convento de Santa Teresa Avila in Castile, Spain.
Bottom: Convent of Santa Teresa in Avila, Spain

23 Galileo Galilei

At a time when philosophers made their mark by discussing the works of Aristotle, who set the bar for science and philosophy, Galileo Galilei believed in observing nature under specific controlled conditions and then using mathematics to describe what happened.

Contrary to what Aristotle taught, Galileo showed that bodies of different weights fall at the same velocity. Despite his controversial approach, Galileo became the chair of mathematics at the University of Padua, known for freedom of thought in study and teaching, where he explored and taught physics for eighteen years.

In 1609, Galileo created a telescope, using information he learned about a device to make faraway objects appear closer. When he turned his new invention toward the night sky, what he observed astounded him.

At this time, conventional wisdom supported Ptolemy's view that the earth was the unmoving center of the solar system. However, Galileo's telescope revealed that Nicholas Copernicus's century-old heliocentric theory (which holds that the earth moves around the sun) was correct.

The church viewed Galileo's observations as heresy, and church leaders cautioned him not to teach or write about his theory. As a scientist, Galileo was defiant, and he refused to acknowledge that what he believed was contrary to the Bible. He stressed that mankind could not fully understand the Bible, and quoted a cardinal in a famous letter, "The Bible shows the way to go to heaven, not the way the heavens go."

He went on to state, "One must not, in my opinion, contradict this statement and block the way of freedom of philosophizing about things of the world and of nature, as if they had all already been discovered and disclosed with certainty."

When faced with the threat of execution as a heretic, Galileo, at age seventy, held fast to his suppositions and spent the rest of his life under house arrest. In his final years, he published a collection of his earlier work, *Dialogue Concerning Two New Sciences*. Not long after he completed the book, he went blind.

In 1981, the Catholic Church ordered a commission to review Galileo's case, and eleven years later, it acknowledged the errors made in judging Galileo as a heretic. In 1992, Pope John Paul II said theologians during Galileo's time did not recognize the distinction between the Bible and interpretations of the Bible. "This led them unduly to transpose into the realm of the doctrine of the faith, a question which in fact pertained to scientific investigation," the pope determined.

Despite his controversies with the church, Galileo viewed himself as a Christian, stating that when the Bible seems to contradict science, "it becomes the office of wise expounders to labor till they find how to make those passages of Holy Writ concordant with these conclusions." ∎

Left: Galileo's telescope, 1610

24 William Shakespeare

French author and playwright Victor Hugo once observed, "England has two books, one which she has made, the other which has made her—Shakespeare and the Bible."

As it turns out, William Shakespeare was deeply influenced by the Bible as well. Many scholars believe that English playwright William Shakespeare grew up listening to the words of the Bible—primarily the Geneva Bible—during services at his local Anglican church. He frequently integrated themes from the Bible and allusions to the Bible into his plays and sonnets. One estimate is that he made 1,200 biblical references in his work, more than any other Elizabethan playwright.

One example, based on 1 Samuel 3:2, comes from *1 Henry VI*: "His eyes began to wax dim, that he could not see" (KJV), where Shakespeare uses the phrase "wax dim." Another example is act 4, scene 1 of his play *Macbeth*, where Shakespeare paraphrases the biblical phrase "laughed thee to scorn" from 2 Kings 19:21 (KJV): "Be bloody, bold, and resolute; laugh to scorn / The power of man, for none of woman born / Shall harm Macbeth."

The play *King Lear* showcases Shakespeare's affinity for the story of Job. Lear's words "Thou'lt come no more" echo Job 7:9-10, which says, "He that goeth down to the grave shall come up no more. He shall return no more" (KJV). The "Non Nobis, Domine" ("Not to us, O Lord") hymn, which is based on Psalm 115:1, appears in Shakespeare's *Henry V* when King Henry V says, "O God,

thy arm was here; and not to us, but to thy arm alone, ascribe we all!"

Additional references to Job are found in plays such as *The Merry Wives of Windsor*, *Julius Caesar*, and others. But, in his typically wry and witty style, Shakespeare also had one of his characters observe that "The devil can cite Scripture for his purpose" (*The Merchant of Venice*, act 1, scene 3).

Shakespeare subtly refers to the Bible's Song of Solomon in many plays and poems. An example is Romeo's words to Juliet in act 2, scene 2 of *Romeo and Juliet*, which reference Song of Solomon 2:10–12: "With love's light wings did I o'er-perch these walls; / For stony limits cannot hold love out, And what love can do that dares love attempt; / Therefore thy kinsmen are no stop to me."

British scholar David Crystal observed, "No other single source [as the Bible] has provided the [English] language with so many idiomatic expressions. Shakespeare is the nearest. . . . However, when it comes to idioms, the Bible reigns definitely supreme." ∎

Top: William Shakespeare
Left: William Shakespeare birthplace in Stratford Upon Avon, UK

25 James I of England

King James I (the only son of Mary, Queen of Scots, and her second husband, Henry Stuart, Lord Darnley) ruled Scotland from the time he was a baby until 1625 as James VI, and he ruled England, Ireland, and Scotland from 1603 as James I until his death.

Calling himself the "king of Great Britain," James advocated the divine right of kings, which did not sit well with Parliament and eventually set the stage for the rebellion that took place against Charles I, his successor.

However, James's most enduring legacy is the Bible translation that bears his name, the King James Version of the Bible. The best-selling Bible translation and perhaps the best-selling book of all time, the King James Bible was completed in 1611 following seven years of work by a unique team of more than fifty scholars.

King James I assembled the Hampton Court Conference in 1604, which proposed to create a new revision of the Bishop's Bible. James wanted no marginal notes and asked for a single uniform translation.

Hailed as a work of literary genius, the King James Version (KJV) has had an amazing impact on the development of English language. Many of the words and phrases we use today were popularized by this the widely read and beloved translation.

Here are a just few examples: *by the skin of your teeth* (Job 19:20); a *broken heart* (Psalm 34:18); *go the extra mile* (Mathew 5:41); *the good Samaritan* (Luke 10:25–37); and *getting to the root of the matter* (Job 19:28).

"Without the King James Bible, there would have been no *Paradise Lost*, no *Pilgrim's Progress*, no Handel's *Messiah*, no Negro spirituals, and no Gettysburg Address," observed Oxford scholar Alister McGrath. "Without this Bible, the culture of the English-speaking world would have been immeasurably impoverished." ∎

Top left: Gold laurel coin, minted in the reign of James I. English
Right: James I (1566-1625), King of England, 1603-25, Portrait

26 John Selden

The great English poet John Milton once called John Selden "the chief of learned men reputed in this land."

As a lawyer and a scholar, Selden fought against the tyranny of English kings throughout the first half of the seventeenth century. His work was found in the libraries of many of America's Founding Founders, who appealed to his viewpoints in defense of their liberties.

Interestingly, it is a lighter work, called *Table Talk*, that is Selden's most well-known legacy. Published after his death in 1698, *Table Talk* is a collection of conversations Selden had with other scholars and notable people of his day, such as Ben Johnson.

The book shows the witty side of a scholarly man, such as the following comments: "Humility is a virtue all preach, none practice; and yet everybody is content to hear." He refers to the church this way: "A glorious Church is like a magnificent feast; there is all the variety that may be, but every one chooses out a dish or two that he likes, and lets the rest alone: how glorious soever the Church is, every one chooses out of it his own religion, by which he governs himself, and lets the rest alone."

Selden began his legal career in 1612 and soon after began writing on legal subjects as well as on the history of government in Britain. In 1617, he wrote *De diis Syris Syntagmata*, a book about polytheism in the Middle East. Throughout his career, he wrote extensively on Jewish law, for which he learned Hebrew and consulted numerous rabbinical texts as well as the Bible. This research outside the English tradition helped supply him with a comprehensive framework for his justification of English common law.

Selden also turned to the Bible for his personal reflections. "There is no book on which we can rest in a dying moment but the Bible," he said in *Table Talk*. ■

Left: Portrait of John Selden

27 Anne Hutchinson

In many ways, Anne Hutchinson was ahead of her time. Intelligent, opinionated, and unafraid of speaking her mind, Hutchinson did not always fit in well with the conservative, Puritan lifestyle of the Massachusetts Bay Colony.

The daughter of a minster, Hutchinson was well versed in the Bible. She later trained as a midwife and a nurse in England. When she and her family settled in Boston in 1634, she hosted lively discussion groups in her home, mostly centered on the sermons of Reverend John Cotton. Hutchinson emphasized the individual's relationship with God, stressing personal revelation over institutionalized observances—views that challenged religious orthodoxy in Massachusetts Bay Colony.

Three-time Massachusetts governor John Winthrop described Hutchinson as "a woman of haughty and fierce carriage, of a nimble wit and active spirit, and a very voluble tongue, more bold than a man."

In 1636, Hutchinson argued that Puritan ministers were teaching that salvation was dependent on good works rather than on God's grace, which was contrary to Puritan teaching. Her charges angered church leaders, and Winthrop charged Hutchinson with sedition and heresy.

During her 1637 trial, Hutchinson defended herself. When she was criticized for teaching the Bible in public, for instance, Hutchinson quoted from the Bible's book of Titus, which instructs older women to teach younger women. Hutchinson did not win her case, however, and she was banished from the colony.

Roger Williams was sympathetic to her position and gave she and her family refuge in the Colony of Rhode Island. She later moved to New York, where she was killed in 1643 in an attack by Siwanoy Indians. ■

Top: Anne Hutchinson, preaching in her house in Boston, Massachusetts, 1637. Illustration by Howard Pyle, 1883

28

John Eliot

As a Puritan pastor in the New World in the seventeenth century, John Eliot followed a lot of rules. For example, he preferred one—just one—plain dish for his dinner. He shunned long hair for men, tobacco, and wigs. And he was extremely frugal.

However, Eliot differed from many of his peers in that he was intrigued by the Native Americans in and around the Massachusetts Bay Colony, and he wanted to help them. Although many scholars trace the modern missionary movement to William Carey's trip to India in 1792, Eliot was bringing the Bible to Native Americans in Massachusetts 150 years earlier.

Eliot is also associated with two big "firsts." He is responsible for the first book printed in the British colonies—the *Bay Psalm Book* in 1640—and, along with Native American assistants, the first Bible printed in America—a translation of the Bible into Wôpanâak, for the Algonquin Indians, saying, "Until we have Bibles, we are not furnished to carry the Gospel unto them for we have no means to carry religion thither, saving the Scriptures."

Born in Widford, Hertfordshire, England, Eliot traveled to the New World in 1631 and lived first in Boston and then in Roxbury, Massachusetts. He visited Algonquin villages and learned their language.

Nicknamed the "apostle of the American Indian," Eliot fought in court for Algonquin property rights, argued for clemency for convicted Algonquin prisoners, established schools for the tribe's children, and fought against slavery of Native Americans. He also translated almost two dozen books into native tongues.

By 1674, Eliot's influence gave rise to the term *praying Indians*, which describes Native Americans who had converted to Christianity. However, during King Philip's War (1675–1676) between the Wampanoag tribe and the English, the English mistrusted the Algonquins and many "praying Indians" were killed or imprisoned. In addition, most copies of Eliot's Bible translation were destroyed.

After the conflict, Eliot continued his work, ministering to the remaining Algonquins and other bands of Indians until his death in 1690. Reports of "praying Indians" continued into the early eighteenth century. ◾

Top: America map dated 1631 showing North and South America
Left: John Eliot: Preacher to the Indians in New England. Unidentified artist

29 Rembrandt

At a time when his contemporaries painted mostly still lifes, landscapes, and portraits, Rembrandt Harmenszoon van Rijn—known simply as Rembrandt—created more than 300 works with biblical themes.

The Dutch painter and etcher brought many scenes from the Bible to life in stunning detail, capturing the humanity of his subjects with his unique method of rendering faces. His use of light and shadows, particularly around the eyes of his figures, helps the viewer see a living, thinking mind behind the face. As a result, in his scenes from the Bible, Rembrandt gives us an enduring and intimate look at how he perceives ordinary people who were touched by the divine.

Rembrandt's Bible-themed paintings bring to life such varied stories as the mysterious handwriting on the wall at *Belshazzar's Feast* (Daniel 5:1–30), the moment the strong man's eyes were gouged out in *The Blinding of Samson* (Judges 16:21), and the time Jesus's disciples feared for their lives in *Christ in a Storm on the Sea of Galilee* (Luke 8:22–25).

Rembrandt did not keep a diary, but we can get a glimpse into his life and his mind-set in the way he painted himself into many of these biblical scenes. For example, in *The Raising of the Cross*, Rembrandt painted

himself as the primary person erecting the cross of Jesus. His contemporary clothing suggests the personal responsibility he felt for the crucifixion.

Rembrandt completed *The Return of the Prodigal Son*, considered by many to be his masterpiece, only a year before he died. In the painting, which is more than eight feet tall and six feet wide, he portrays the wayward son (Luke 15:11–32) who has returned home seeking his father's mercy. With his use of lighting, color, and shadow, Rembrandt aimed to give the painting the emotional tenderness that communicates the themes of forgiveness and love in Jesus's parable of the prodigal son. ∎

REPUBLIQUE CENTRAFRICAINE
90F
Le Christ dans la tempête
POSTE AERIENNE
REMBRANDT 1606-1669

Top: Rembrandt Laughing, by Rembrandt van Rijn, c. 1628, Dutch painting, oil on copper.
Left: A stamp shows a painting of the artist Rembrandt "Christ in the Storm on the Sea of Galilee"

37

30 John Milton

Of Man's first disobedience and the fruit
Of that forbidden tree, whose mortal taste
Brought death into the world, and all our woe,
With loss of Eden, till one greater Man [Jesus],
Restore us and regain the blissful seat,
Sing, O heavenly Muse . . .

These are the opening lines of Paradise Lost, an epic poem by John Milton.

Paradise Lost is not the only time that Milton used biblical themes in his writings. His drama *Samson Agonistes* ("Samson the Athlete") retells the story of Samson recorded in the Bible's book of Judges, chapters 13 through 16. *Samson Agonistes* describes Samson after he was captured and blinded by the Philistines. Interestingly, Milton was blind himself when he wrote it in 1671.

Born in London, John Milton began writing poetry when he was only nine years old. His plans to become a clergyman went by the wayside when he became involved in politics. He wrote pamphlets in support of Oliver Cromwell during the English Civil War, and he later held the post of secretary for foreign languages in Cromwell's government.

It was during this time that Milton began to lose his eyesight, and he was fully blind by 1651. He then dictated his poems to a secretary.

Many scholars put John Milton on par with William Shakespeare as the most influential writer in the history of the English language. He also wrote *Paradise Regained*, published in 1671, based on the Gospel of Luke's story of the temptation of Jesus in the wilderness. ∎

Top: John Milton, author of *Paradise Lost*, engraving depicting him at age 21, 1731

31 Algernon Sidney

Samuel Adams referred to him a patriot.

Thomas Jefferson said his *Discourses Concerning Government* "may be considered as those generally approved by our fellow citizens of this, and the United States."

A group of Virginians, including Patrick Henry, gave his name (along with John Hampden's) to Hampden-Sydney College, which he helped establish in 1775.

Yet many Americans have never heard of Algernon Sidney, an English philosopher who influenced the Founding Fathers.

A member of the Long Parliament, so named because it was in session for eleven years, in the climactic phase of the English Civil War, and also a member of the Protectorate under Oliver Cromwell, who ruled England as a republic after the execution of the King Charles I, Sidney was a strong advocate of a republican form of government. He was staunchly opposed to the concept of the divine right of kings.

In his most famous work, *Discourses Concerning Government*, Sidney argued that God had enabled humans to form governments according to reason. He maintained that governments should be accountable to the people, and the people should be involved in changing the governments.

He frequently cited the Bible to prove his points. For example, Sidney used Joshua's role in the Israelite commonwealth (as described in Jeremiah 30:20–21) as a political model. "Having seen what government God

did not ordain," Sidney wrote, "it may be reasonable to examine the nature of the government which he did ordain; and we shall easily find that it consisted of three parts, besides the magistrates of the several tribes and cities. They had a chief magistrate, who was called judge or captain, as Joshua, Gideon, and others, a council of seventy chosen men, and the general assemblies of the people."

Sidney was executed in 1683, partially because he was accused of believing in the right of revolution. However, his influence continued nearly a century later as the American Founders studied his work. ∎

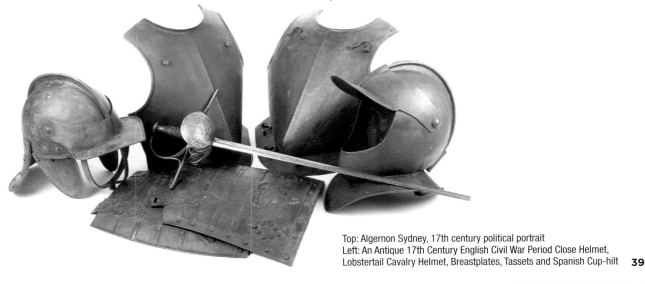

Top: Algernon Sydney, 17th century political portrait
Left: An Antique 17th Century English Civil War Period Close Helmet, Lobstertail Cavalry Helmet, Breastplates, Tassets and Spanish Cup-hilt **39**

34 George Frideric Handel

A legend states that King George II of England was so moved when he heard the "Hallelujah" chorus of George Frideric Handel's *Messiah* that he stood during its London premiere. Not to be left sitting when the king was standing, the entire audience stood as well. Today the tradition of standing during the famous chorus continues.

Messiah, an oratorio that tells the story of Jesus, is Handel's most famous composition. With a text based entirely on the Bible, *Messiah* is performed around the world, especially at Christmas and at Easter.

Handel composed *Messiah* in an intense three- to four-week period in late summer 1741. Another legend regarding the piece is that his assistant discovered Handel in tears during his work on the chorus, saying, "I did think I saw heaven open, and saw the very face of God."

The German-born English Baroque composer wrote many other works based directly on the Bible. He composed music depicting the Israelites escaping Egyptian slavery from Exodus, the story of Samson and Delilah, the story of King Solomon, and the story of Queen Esther.

Handel also composed music for Britain's royal family. Two of his most famous royal works are *Water Music* (so-called as it was for entertaining the royal family on the banks of the River Thames) and *Music for the Royal Fireworks*.

Handel's *Zadok the Priest* has been the official coronation music for British monarchs since King George II in 1714. The composition is based on the events of 1 Kings 1:38–40, when Zadok anoints King Solomon with oil. Written for both choir and orchestra, it ends with the famous phrase "God Save the King, Long Live the King, May the King Live Forever." ∎

Bottom: George Frideric Handel, composer - by Balthasar Denner, 1728

35 Johann Sebastian Bach

Listeners are still in awe when they hear musicians play a composition by Johann Sebastian Bach. The baroque-era composer, known for "Toccata and Fugue in D Minor," The Well-Tempered Clavier," "Mass in B Minor" and the "Brandenburg Concertos," is in a class of his own because of his complex and stylistic music.

Bach, who was born in Eisenach, Thuringia, Germany, came from a long line of musicians. His father, who served as the town musician, taught him to play the violin. By the time Bach reached his tenth birthday, however, he was an orphan. His older brother, who worked as a church organist, took him in, taught him music, and enrolled him in a local school.

With his natural talent, Bach soon was excelling at the organ and the violin, and it was not long before he won a position as a court musician for the Duke Johann Ernst in Weimar. His growing skill landed him a series of important positions as organist and music instructor at large churches. However, Bach's complex rhythms and melodies sometimes clashed with what his employers and patrons wanted.

Raised as a Lutheran, Bach was heavily influenced by Martin Luther and owned two copies of the Luther Bible, in which he wrote annotations for certain scriptures in the margins. Bach considered his music a form of worship, and he wrote a dedication to God on almost all his musical scores. Cantatas, which are pieces for orchestra, choir, and soloists that are connected with religious themes, made up nearly half of his musical output. He also wrote masses, oratorios, and chorales for church music.

Interestingly, Bach was thought of more as a musician than as a composer during his lifetime. In fact, it wasn't until many years after his death when some classical and romantic composers, such as Mozart, Beethoven, and Mendelssohn, shared their admiration of his work that people began to appreciate Bach's magnificent music.

Today, his "The Passion of Saint Matthew," has been called "the supreme cultural achievement of all Western civilization." Even philosopher Friedrich Nietzsche once said of the piece, "One who has completely forgotten Christianity truly hears it here as gospel."

Bach's "Jesu, Joy of Man's Desiring" is commonly performed today at wedding ceremonies and during Christmas and Easter services.

Through Bach's music, he exposed the Bible to various parts of the world. For example, Christian conductor M. Suzuki stated, "Bach works as a missionary among our people in Japan. After each concert, people crowd the podium wishing to talk to me about topics that are normally taboo in our society—death, for example. Then they inevitably ask me what "hope" means to Christians. I believe that Bach has already converted tens of thousands of Japanese to the Christian faith."

Keisuke, a Japanese musicologist, traveled to Bach's church in Germany to study Bach's cantatas. As a result, he said to a pastor, "It is not enough to read Christian texts. I want to be a Christian myself. Please baptize me."

In his book, *Bach: Music in the Castle of Heaven*, the conductor John Eliot Gardiner wrote of Bach's influence: "Beethoven tells us what a terrible struggle it is to transcend human frailties and to aspire to the Godhead; and Mozart shows us the kind of music we might hope to hear in heaven. But it is Bach, making music in the Castle of Heaven, who gives us the voice of God—in human form. He is the one who blazes a trail, showing us how to overcome our imperfections through the perfections of his music: to make divine things human and human things divine." ■

Top: Johann Sebastian Bach (1685-1750) in 1746. Portrait by Elias Gottlieb Haussman.

36 Benjamin Franklin

As a writer, printer, inventor, diplomat, humorist, political theorist, postmaster, and scientist, Benjamin Franklin was the Renaissance Man of America's Founding Fathers.

As a scientist and inventor, he invented the lightning rod, the Franklin stove, and bifocal glasses. As a writer, he published *Poor Richard's Almanac*, giving us his timeless wisdom in such phrases as, "Speak little, do much"; "A friend in need is a friend indeed"; "Lost time is never found again"; and "There are no gains without pains."

As a statesman, Franklin served as the first US postmaster, minister to England and France, and a representative to the Continental Congress, where he assisted in the development of the Constitution.

He opened the first public library in America and the first public hospital in Philadelphia, founded the American Philosophical Society, and was one of the first people to call for a union of the American colonies in 1754.

Before the Revolutionary War, Franklin served as a colonial agent in London for several years. Afterward, he represented the new United States in France, helping to negotiate a treaty of alliance and support, as well as facilitating the final peace treaty with Great Britain in 1783. In 1787, Franklin served as the elder statesman at the Constitutional Convention. Before his death in 1790, he became one of the leading advocates for the abolition of slavery.

Franklin believed that religion was important to the moral well-being of society. Some historians have suggested that Franklin was a Deist, believing that God created the universe and then left it alone to develop. However, Franklin's speeches and writings suggest otherwise.

For example, in a speech at the Constitutional Convention in 1787, he referenced the Bible (Matthew 10:29–30) by saying, "I have lived, Sir, a long time and the longer I live, the more convincing proofs I see of this truth—that God governs in the affairs of men. And if a sparrow cannot fall to the ground without his notice, is it probable that an empire can rise without his aid? We have been assured, Sir, in the sacred writings that 'except the Lord build they labor in vain that build it.'"

Along with Thomas Jefferson and John Adams, Franklin also was involved in proposing a seal for

his new country, which depicts the free Israelites—representing the Americans—on one side of the Red Sea, with Pharaoh and the Egyptians—representing King George and England—on the other side.

Franklin supported the evangelist George Whitefield, one of the main figures in the first Great Awakening, a religious revival that swept throughout the colonies. In his *Autobiography*, Franklin described how he initially planned to contribute nothing to Whitefield's ministry but ended up giving him all the money he had in his pocket. Franklin also printed broadsides for George Whitefield. ■

Top: Benjamin Franklin, by Jean-Baptiste Greuze (copy) 1777, French painting, oil on canvas. Franklin sat for the painter Jean-Baptiste Greuze in 1777, soon after his arrival in France.
Bottom: Benjamin Franklin signature, illustration

Benjamin's Franklin kite in a dangerous electrical storm

39 George Washington

He has been called the American Moses and the father of America. In a eulogy read at his funeral, his friend Henry "Light Horse Harry" Lee described him as "First in war, first in peace, and first in the hearts of his countrymen."

This man is George Washington, America's first president and the general who led the colonies to independence from Great Britain. Both the decisions he made and the character he exemplified throughout his career in the military and in the government had far-reaching effects on the new nation he served.

As early as his first day in office, Washington began establishing traditions. In 1789, as he took the oath of office before a cheering crowd in New York City, Washington placed his hand on the pages of an open Bible. Several presidents have followed that custom since then.

Born in Westmoreland County, Virginia, to a colonial plantation owner, Washington rose to prominence as a military leader during the French and Indian War. He represented Virginia at the First Continental Congress in 1774, when tensions between America and Great Britain were at fever pitch. In 1775, at the Second Continental Congress, Washington was nominated as commander-in-chief of the new Continental Army.

Despite calls for him to become the first American king after the War for Independence, Washington chose to leave the limelight and return home to his beloved Mount Vernon. He answered the call of his country again, however, in 1787 to serve as president of the Constitutional Convention. He was subsequently elected the first president of the United States, serving two terms. Declining calls to serve a third term, he once again returned home, where he died just three years later.

Washington was ambiguous about his spiritual life, but he regularly appealed to "an all-powerful Providence" to guide him, his troops, and his nation. In his speeches and letters, he cited and referenced the Bible frequently. In his 1783 "Circular to the States," for instance, he referred to the Bible as the "light of Revelation" and called it the most important contributing factor to the events that produced the new American nation.

In his first inaugural address, Washington said, "It would be peculiarly improper to omit in this first official act my fervent supplications to that Almighty Being who rules over the universe, who presides in the councils of nations, and whose providential aids can supply every human defect . . . the propitious smiles of Heaven can never be expected on a nation that disregards the eternal rules of right and order which Heaven itself has ordained." ■

40 John Adams

John Adams once said, "But what do we mean by the American Revolution? Do we mean the American war? The Revolution was effected before the war commenced. The Revolution was in the minds and hearts of the people."

Adams was our nation's first vice president and our second president. He also was the father of our sixth president, John Quincy Adams. However, these titles would mean nothing if Adams had not first helped lead the revolution "in the minds and hearts of the people."

Born in Quincy, Massachusetts, to a family descended from original Massachusetts Bay colonists, Adams received his undergraduate degree and master's degrees from Harvard and became a respected lawyer. Despite his disdain for increasing British control over the colonies, he served as the defense attorney for the British soldiers involved in the Boston Massacre.

Later he served on the first and second Continental Congresses and helped draft the US Declaration of Independence. Adams represented the new nation in diplomatic posts in Europe, helping to secure alliances, loans, and peace. He served as George Washington's vice president for two terms and then succeeded him as president.

A prolific writer, Adams filled his books, journals, and letters with biblical quotes and allusions. "The Bible is the best book in the world and for that reason among a thousand others, I want to know more about it," he wrote in a letter in 1813. ■

Top left: The birthplace of John Adams in Quincy, MA
Top right: John Adams as Vice-President during the George Washington Presidency. Ca. 1795.

41 Thomas Jefferson

Scientist, botanist, political thinker, musician, writer, university founder. Thomas Jefferson had a long list of talents and accomplishments to add to his reputation as a Founding Father and president of the United States.

As the writer of the Declaration of Independence, Jefferson became the voice of the new democracy. He also championed the nation's geographic expansion through the Louisiana Purchase and the Lewis and Clark expedition during his presidency.

Born in Albemarle County, Virginia, Jefferson inherited 5,000 acres of land from his father and social status from his mother. He studied law at the College of William and Mary and soon became involved with the growing protests the colonies had against England. He served in the Virginia legislature and the Continental Congress and as governor of Virginia. He later served as ambassador to France, as the first US Secretary of State, as the second Vice President, and as the third President. After retiring from politics, he founded the University of Virginia, not far from his beloved mountaintop home, Monticello.

A true representation of the eighteenth-century Age of Enlightenment, Jefferson was influenced by Deism, the belief in a God that does not interfere with the universe he created. He was an early and strong advocate for religious freedom and the separation of church and state in America.

In both of his presidential inaugural addresses, Jefferson acknowledged God and directed prayers to him. He also used the idea of the United States as a "Promised Land," a new society whose fundamental principle was human liberty.

A lifelong student of the Bible, Jefferson was skeptical about the accuracy of the Gospels. He used a cut-and-paste method with a razor blade and glue to create his unique, edited version of the Bible, featuring selected teachings of Jesus. After studying the New Testament in Latin, Greek, French, and King James English, Jefferson completed his eighty-four-page *The Life and Moral of Jesus of Nazareth* (commonly referred to as the Jefferson Bible) in 1820.

Jefferson wrote that the book was "the result of a life of enquiry and reflection, and very different from that anti-Christian system, imputed to me by those who know nothing of my opinions." ∎

Left: Thomas Jefferson 1743-1826, artist unknown

42 Abigail Adams

"My pen is always freer than my tongue," wrote Abigail Adams to her husband in 1775. "I have wrote [sic] many things to you that I suppose I never could have talked."

For more than forty years, including periods of long separations that were key to the founding of the United States, Adams poured out her heart—and her considerable intellect—to her husband. Her letters would shed an interesting light on eighteenth-century history no matter who she was. They are filled with politics, social mores, humor, and love.

However, since Adams was the wife of the second president of the United States—John Adams—and the mother of the sixth—John Quincy Adams—her letters are historical gold. During her husband's frequent absences to tend to his business as a lawyer and as a politician, Adams reported to him about details of her busy life. In addition to being the mother of four children, she ran the family farm in his absence, often dealing with tenants and sometimes buying property.

Her writing reveals her love of reading, which was instilled in her by her parents, and the close bond she shared with her husband. Her wartime letters are a combination of local news and strong political commentary. In March 1776, while John Adams attended the Continental Congress, she wrote, "I desire you would remember the ladies, and be more generous and favorable to them than your ancestors. Do not put such unlimited power into the hands of the husbands."

Abigail Adams was born to religious parents in Weymouth, Massachusetts. Her father was a Congregationalist minister, and she grew up reading and memorizing the Bible. She often referred to the Bible in her letters. For example, in a 1775 letter about the growing threat of war, she wrote to her husband, "We live in continual expectation of hostilities. Scarcely a day that does not produce some; but like good Nehemiah, having made our prayer unto God and set the people with their swords, their spears, and their bows, we will say unto them "Be not ye afraid of them; remember the Lord, who is great and terrible, and fight for your brethren, your sons, and your daughters, your wives and your houses (Nehemiah 4:14)."

Adams also wrote to her children and her grandchildren, sprinkling them with advice and frequently referencing the Bible. In a letter to John Quincy, she wrote, "Adhere to those religious sentiments and principles which were early instilled into your mind and remember that you are accountable to your Maker for all your words and actions." ∎

Top: Abigail Smith Adams, by Gilbert Stuart, c. 1800-15, American painting, oil on canvas.
Left: Interior of "Peacefield" - the home of John and Abigail Adams, Adams National Historical Park in Braintree, Quincy, MA.

43 James Madison

James Madison's amazing résumé includes writing the first drafts of the US Constitution, cowriting the Federalist Papers, sponsoring the Bill of Rights, serving as President Thomas Jefferson's secretary of state, and serving two terms as US president.

Born and raised on a Virginia plantation, Montpelier, Madison was the oldest of twelve children. At age eighteen, he left home to attend the College of New Jersey (now Princeton University). When Virginia began preparing for the Revolutionary War, Madison was appointed a colonel in the Orange County, Virginia militia. Due primarily to poor health, he gave up his military career for politics, and in 1776, he represented Orange County at the Virginia Constitutional Convention.

In 1780, Madison represented his state in the Continental Congress in Philadelphia. He returned to the Virginia assembly in 1783 to work on a religious freedom statute but was soon be called back to help create a new constitution. In 1786, the Virginia Legislature, under Madison's leadership, permanently ended the state's religious establishment by passing a bill for religious freedom.

Madison believed religious freedom was an individual's right from birth, and he played a key role in developing the idea of religious liberty in America. As a young man, Madison was enthusiastically religious, writing of the need to "have our names enrolled in the annals of Heaven." As he grew older, however, he became tight-lipped about his religious views, even in his private letters.

Despite this reticence, Madison revealed that he was deeply influenced by the Bible. For example, he emphasized the idea that humanity is flawed and that being flawed meant two things: government was necessary, but that government must be limited and controlled. Based on this reasoning, he encouraged the system of checks and balances that still makes up the foundation of American government. In 1789, he took the lead in steering a bill through the First Federal Congress that would explicitly list the rights of American citizens, including rights regarding religion.

Madison frequently used biblical metaphors to make his points. For example, he used Jesus's differentiation between "God and Caesar" to support his arguments for religious liberty (Matthew 22:21: "Render to Caesar the things that are Caesar's, and to God the things that are God's.") He also asserted that religious liberty would lead to the faster spread of Christianity and a more heartfelt adherence to it.

As president, Madison signed a federal bill in 1812 to exempt Bible societies from paying duties on imports on products needed to print Bibles. ∎

Left: James Madison, by Gilbert Stuart , 1821, American painting, oil on canvas.
Bottom: US Constitution

44 Wolfgang Amadeus Mozart

A rare musical prodigy, Wolfgang Amadeus Mozart could adeptly play several instruments and compose music at the age of five. Until his death at the age of thirty-five, the Austrian artist went on to compose a dizzying array of operas, symphonies, concertos, and sonatas that shaped classical music.

Born in Salzburg, Austria, and raised as a Catholic, Mozart began entertaining European nobility and church officials as a young child. His work belied his years in its emotion and sophistication.

For much of his life, Mozart was employed by church officials to write sacred music. For example, his 1773 motet *Exsultate, jubilate* ("Rejoice, Be Glad"), written when he was only seventeen, was inspired in part by Psalm 81. As an older adult, he also wrote such works as *Davide penitente* (Penitent David), which premiered in March 1785 in Vienna. It was inspired by the story in 2 Samuel 12:15–23 of David's grief over the death of his firstborn child and his repentance for his adulterous relationship with Bathsheba.

Some of Mozart's later liturgical works include the Great Mass in C minor, a large-scale work written for the Salzburg Cathedral in 1783; the *Ave Verum Corpus*, written in Baden in 1791, and the *Requiem Mass*, which he did not complete before his death.

Mozart led a lavish lifestyle, one that, largely due to his mismanagement of money, he could not afford. By 1790, he described his wife, his children, and himself living in dire financial circumstances. By this time, he was also ill, suffering from what historians believe was kidney disease.

With the success of his opera *The Magic Flute*, however, the composer was beginning to turn his life around when his illness took his life. His music left an enduring legacy, however, influencing many composers, including Richard Wagner and Peter Tchaikovsky in the nineteenth century and Igor Stravinsky and Sergei Prokofiev in the twentieth century. ◼

Top: Wolfgang Amadeus Mozart (1756-1791)
Bottom: Panoramic view of Salzburg skyline with Festung Hohensalzburg and river Salzach, Salzburger Land, Austria

45 William Wilberforce

At a time when the slave trade was firmly entrenched in the British economy, William Wilberforce dedicated his life to stopping it. "So enormous, so dreadful, so irremediable did the trade's wickedness appear that my own mind was completely made up for abolition," he wrote. "Let the consequences be what they would: I from this time determined that I would never rest until I had effected its abolition."

Born in England into a family of wealth, Wilberforce studied at Cambridge University. There, he became close friends with William Pitt the Younger, who was later British prime minister during the French Revolutionary and Napoleonic Wars. Both men became members of Parliament in the House of Commons in 1780.

However, Wilberforce later acknowledged, "The first years in Parliament I did nothing—nothing to any purpose. My own distinction was my darling object." In 1786, he experienced a spiritual rebirth and found new purpose in fighting the slave trade.

As a member of what became known as the Clapham Sect, he assisted the Society for Effecting the Abolition of the Slave Trade and the Proclamation Society, which sought to prevent the publication of obscenity, presenting their cause to the House of Commons.

Wilberforce earned the nickname "the prime minister of a cabinet of philanthropists." He donated one-fourth of his income to the poor and helped establish parachurch groups like the Church Missionary Society, the Society for Bettering the Cause of the Poor, the Foreign Bible Society, and the Antislavery Society.

In his 1797 book *A Practical View of the Prevailing Religious System*, Wilberforce wrote, "The truth is, their opinions on these subjects are not formed form the perusal of the word of God. The Bible lies unopened; and they would by wholly ignorant of its contents . . . how different, nay, in many respects, how contradictory would be the two systems of mere morals of which the one should be formed from the commonly received maxims of the Christian world, and the other from the study of the holy Scriptures!"

The efforts of Wilberforce and other abolitionists were finally successful in 1807, when Parliament outlawed the slave trade, and again in 1833, when it outlawed slavery. Plagued by ill health most of his life, Wilberforce died three days later. ■

Top: William Wilberforce (1759-1833), artist unknown
Left: William Wilberforce and slaves, stained glass window.
Clapham, London, England, Holy Trinity Church

46 Ludwig van Beethoven

Da-Da-Da-DUM. Almost anyone anywhere, whether a music lover or not, can recognize the first four notes of Beethoven's Fifth Symphony.

According to Matthew Guerrieri, author of *The First Four Notes: Beethoven's Fifth and the Human Imagination,* "The most common story that is told is that Beethoven allegedly said that the opening of the symphony was supposedly symbolizing fate knocking at the door. . . . The other story going around at the time that Beethoven wrote it was that he had gotten the opening motif from the song of a bird . . . to Beethoven, that actually would have been a fairly noble way of getting a musical idea."

Ludwig van Beethoven's innovative piano sonatas, chamber music, and symphonies are an essential part of the canon of Western classical music and continue to be performed around the world. Many consider the German pianist as the greatest composer of all time. His

accomplishments are even more amazing, considering he wrote some of his most important works after he was completely deaf.

Beethoven had a complicated relationship with religion. Many of his letters express a belief in a personal God, and he frequently wrote religious inscriptions on the manuscripts of his compositions. However, toward the end of his life, especially, he seemed to have become more of a Deist.

Many of his compositions draw heavily on biblical text and allusions to the Bible. For example, he depicted the suffering of Christ in the Garden of Gethsemane in his oratorio Christ on the Mount of Olives.

His most famous sacred work is the Missa Solemnis. Beethoven is said to have called the deeply personal sounding mass the "crown of my life's work." Written to celebrate the appointment of his friend and patron, the Archduke Rudolph of Austria, as archbishop, the mass revives many older forms of religious music that Beethoven studied and admired. The movements are based on traditional liturgical songs, including the *Sanctus*, which quotes verses from the Psalms and the Gospels: "Benedictus qui venit in nomine Domini! Osanna in excelsis!" (Blessed is he who cometh in the name of the Lord!, Hosanna in the highest!)

Biographers believe Beethoven had plans to write several other masses, including a requiem, but he did not complete them before his death at the age of fifty-six. ∎

Left: Ludwig van Beethoven (1770-1827) in portrait by Carl Jaeger.
Top: Beethoven playing at Wolfgang Amadeus Mozart 's salon, 1787.

47 Elizabeth Fry

Elizabeth Fry was born in Norwich, Norfolk, England to Quaker parents, and she eventually became a Quaker minister.

As a young wife and mother, Fry gave medicine and clothing to London's homeless and helped start a school for nurses called the Sisters of Devonshire Square. She was motivated by the words of Jesus recorded in Matthew 25:36: "I was naked and you clothed me, I was sick and you visited me, I was in prison and you came to me." In 1813, thirty-three-year-old Fry turned her attention to London's prison system.

During visits to Newgate Prison, she was horrified to find women crowded into cells. Multiple women slept, ate, and defecated in the same confined space. Female prisoners who had stolen apples were in the same cells as convicted murderers. In many cases, young children lived in the cells with their mothers, enduring the same squalid conditions.

For the next thirty years, Fry devoted her life to prison reform. She began by providing clean clothes for the women. She also organized classes in basic hygiene, as well as in sewing and quilting so they could earn a living upon release from prison. She even accompanied condemned women to the scaffold to comfort them with prayer.

Officials repeatedly warned her to stay away because the prisons were unsafe and unsanitary. Fry responded that she received her strength from God. Study of the Bible became a mainstay of her prison work. She read the Bible aloud to the prisoners and gave copies to those who could read.

Fry became a respected international leader in prison reform. Through her leadership, strong regulations were introduced, including separate institutions for men and women, female guards for women, housing based on the severity of the crimes, and paid work for prisoners. ■

Top: Elizabeth Fry reading the Bible to prisoners in Newgate, by Jerry Barrett, 1816.
Bottom: Elizabeth Fry, illustration

48 William Holmes McGuffey

Generations of American schoolchildren learned to read, write, and spell with McGuffey Readers. More than 120 million copies of these graded primers were sold between 1836 and 1960, placing the textbooks alongside the Bible and Webster's Dictionary in terms of sales. They are still used in homes and schools today and continue to sell at a rate of about 30,000 copies a year.

The popular books bear the name of American educator William Holmes McGuffey. McGuffey's parents were Protestants who immigrated from Scotland in 1774, bringing their religious beliefs that education should include academic as well as moral instruction.

A bright student who could memorize entire books of the Bible, McGuffey began teaching in small Ohio frontier schools when he was only fourteen. He was known for working eleven hours a day, six days a week. After graduating from college, he married Harriet Spinning, and the couple had five children.

In 1835, a publisher asked McGuffey to put together a progressive series of textbooks for schoolchildren that would teach reading, writing, spelling, and morals. Harriet Beecher Stowe, the author and abolitionist who would later write *Uncle Tom's Cabin*, had recommended McGuffey for the job.

Originally titled Eclectic Readers, McGuffey Readers, as they came to be known, directly state the need of the Bible as a basis for learning and include selections from Shakespeare and sections from the Bible, as well as parables and stories that extoll patriotism, faith in God, family, and good behavior.

In the introduction to his books, McGuffey, referring to himself in the third person, wrote, "For the copious extracts made from the Sacred Scriptures, he makes no apology. Indeed, upon a review of the work, he is not sure but an apology may be due for his not having still more liberally transferred to his pages the chaste simplicity, the thrilling pathos, the living descriptions, and the overwhelming sublimity of the sacred writings." ■

Top left: Antique ca. 1890 photograph, country school with teacher and students. Location unknown.
Top right: William Holmes McGuffey

49 Alexis de Tocqueville

French philosopher Alexis de Tocqueville was fascinated by America. He spent nine months touring the country, and his resulting two-volume *Democracy in America* makes keen observations about nineteenth-century America and the American Experiment in general.

Born into an aristocratic French family, Alexis de Tocqueville's parents were both imprisoned during the Reign of Terror (1793–1794). In Paris, Tocqueville studied law, and he was later appointed a magistrate in Versailles. In 1830, when Louis-Philippe took the throne in France, he and his friend, fellow lawyer Gustave de Beaumont, obtained permission to study the American penal system. In April 1831, they set sail for America.

Tocqueville's writing is filled with interesting social and political observations. They range from his surprise at how early Americans eat breakfast to his warnings that a society of individuals can result in a "tyranny of the majority" in which rights become compromised.

He observed that the pervasiveness of biblical teaching in the United States was essential to the political ideal of equal justice under the law. He observed, "Christianity, which has made all men equal before God, will not flinch to see all citizens equal before the law." In addition, he attributed the idea of human equality directly to the biblical teachings of Jesus when he stated, "Jesus Christ had to come into the world to reveal that all members of the human race were similar and equal by nature." Jesus's teachings followed the Hebrew Bible's idea of developing a political system based on the concept of equality.

Tocqueville saw that the American ideals of democracy and equality were rooted in the Judeo-Christian ethic and that while the ideals of liberty and religion had moved in opposite directions in Europe, they worked well together in the United States. "This [Anglo-American] civilization is the result of two quite distinct ingredients which anywhere else have often ended in war," he wrote, "but which Americans have succeeded somehow to meld together in wondrous harmony, namely the *spirit of religion* and the *spirit of liberty*."

Tocqueville noted that the Bible was an important component of American culture, remarking that a true American is one "who penetrates into the wilds

of the New World with the Bible, an axe, and some newspaper." He also noticed the influence of the Bible on the American penal system. Tocqueville observed that American prisons were providing inmates with copies of the Bible and that many of them had learned to read as a result.

In 1839, Tocqueville reentered French political life as a deputy in the French assembly. He later served briefly as Louis Napoleon's foreign minister before he was ousted because he did not support Napoleon's coup. He was working on his two-volume history of modern France when he died from tuberculosis in 1859. ■

Top: Alexis de Tocqueville, Painting by Théodore Chassériau.

50 Abraham Lincoln

Because his second term as president was cut short by an assassin's bullet, we do not know for certain what Abraham Lincoln considered his greatest accomplishment. We do know that many historians and American citizens consider him one of the greatest presidents.

Not only did Lincoln preserve the Union through victory in the Civil War, but his actions brought American slavery to an end. In 1863, he signed the Emancipation Proclamation and urged the passing of a constitutional amendment prohibiting slavery. (The Thirteenth Amendment passed after his death in 1865.)

As president, he authorized the first Railroad Act, the Homestead Act, and the US Department of Agriculture; he also made Thanksgiving a national holiday. He established land grants for public universities and, ironically, he approved the creation of the Secret Service. Although today, we associate the Secret Service with presidential bodyguards, Lincoln approved the agency to stop currency counterfeiting.

We do know that Lincoln's life was full of the Bible. During his childhood in Kentucky and Indiana, books were scarce, and the Bible was used as a textbook in his small, one-room schoolhouse. In a White House conversation with Senator John B. Henderson, Lincoln said, "I attended . . . a log schoolhouse in Indiana where we had no reading books or grammars, and all our reading was done from the Bible. We stood in a long line and read in turn from it."

As a young man, Lincoln was skeptical about religious orthodoxy. Nevertheless, Lincoln's language was full of references to the Bible, and he appeared to rely more and more on his foundation in the Bible as his political career went on.

For example, Lincoln's famous "house divided against itself cannot stand" analogy from his 1858 Republican nomination speech for the Senate directly references Jesus's words in Luke 11:17, Mark 3:25, and Matthew 12:25. The Gettysburg Address and his Second Inaugural Address also include biblical allusions and quotes.

According to William E. Barton, Lincoln's biographer, the sixteenth president "read the Bible, honored it, quoted it freely, and it became so much a part of him as visibly and permanently to give shape to his literary style and to his habits of thought."

When a group of African Americans from Baltimore presented Lincoln with a Bible in September 1864, he said, "So far as able, within my sphere, I have always acted as I believed to be right and just; and I have done all I could for the good of mankind generally. In letters and documents sent from this office, I have expressed myself better than I now can. In regard to this Great Book, I have but to say, it is the best gift God has given to man." ∎

Left: Acrylic painting of Abraham Lincoln, published on the 100th anniversary of his birth in 1909.

51 Harriet Beecher Stowe

"So, you're the little woman who wrote the book that made this great war!" is how President Abraham Lincoln reportedly greeted novelist and abolitionist Harriet Beecher Stowe upon their meeting in 1862.

Lincoln was referring to Stowe's best-known work, *Uncle Tom's Cabin*. Published in 1852, the novel brought slavery to the forefront of the sensibilities of American readers, many of whom were previously unaware of how brutally slaves were often treated. A contemporary critic called *Uncle Tom's Cabin* "perhaps the most influential novel ever published, a verbal earthquake, an ink-and-paper tidal wave."

Harriet Beecher Stowe was the seventh of twelve children born to Lyman Beecher, a Congregationalist minister, revivalist, and reformer, and Roxana Foote Beecher, a religious woman who died when Stowe was five.

As her mother lay dying, her father repeated the words of Hebrews 12:22–24 (KJV):

"Ye are come unto mount Sion, and unto the city of the living God, the heavenly Jerusalem, and to an innumerable company of angels, to the general assembly and church of the firstborn, . . . and to the spirits of just men made perfect, and to Jesus the mediator of the new covenant, and to the blood of sprinkling, that speaketh better things than that of Abel."

For Stowe, that passage, which became an important one for her family, along with others from the Bible, fueled her desire to do something to stop the institution of slavery. If the slave is invited to come to Jesus, she reasoned, then how can he be bought and sold on an auction block?

Uncle Tom's Cabin was first published as a serial in 1851–1852 in the *National Era*, an anti-slavery newspaper, and then in book form. It sold an astonishing 10,000 copies in one week, more than 300,000 copies in its first year, and one million copies prior to the Civil War—all despite being banned in the South. *Uncle Tom's Cabin* also included quotes and references to the Bible.

Published in twenty-three languages, *Uncle Tom's Cabin* became the best-selling book of the nineteenth century, second only to the Bible. ◼

Top left: *Uncle Tom's Cabin*
Top right: Harriet Beecher Stowe, author of *Uncle Tom's Cabin*

WORDSWORTH CLASSICS
A Tale of Two Cities
CHARLES DICKENS

52 Charles Dickens

Through such memorable characters as the miser Ebenezer Scrooge, the hardworking Bob Cratchit, and the joyous-through-adversity young Tiny Tim, Charles Dickens gave us a timeless story of redemption.

A Christmas Carol, first published in 1843, influenced the modern celebration of Christmas, including the use of the phrase "Merry Christmas." The beloved novella continues to delight people each year in print, stage, and screen versions.

Dickens also wrote *David Copperfield, A Tale of Two Cities, Bleak House, Great Expectations,* and *Our Mutual Friend.* He often explored the struggles and hardships of the poor in Victorian England—a theme he understood firsthand.

Dickens was born into a middle-class London family, and his father held a well-paid position as a clerk in the navy. However, hard times and poor money management brought financial ruin to the family.

At age twelve, Charles Dickens had to leave school to work long hours in a factory while his father served time in debtors' prison. Dickens had the humiliating task of selling his family's treasured books to the local pawn shop. Although things eventually improved for his family,

Dickens was forever marked by these experiences, and he used his writing as a way of championing the poor and oppressed.

Dickens was profoundly influenced by the Bible and the teachings of Jesus. He once wrote, "All my strongest illustrations are derived from the New Testament. All my social abuses are shown as departures from its Spirit. All my good people are humble, charitable, faithful, forgiving, over and over again. I claim them in expressed words as disciples of the Founder of our religion."

As a gift for his own ten children, Dickens wrote a retelling of the life of Jesus from the Gospel of Luke called *The Life of Our Lord.* The little book was passed down by Dickens's descendants and was not published until 1934.

He also gave each of his children a copy of the New Testament when they left home. To one child, he wrote, "I put a New Testament among your books, for the very same reasons, and with the very same hopes that made me write an easy account of it for you, when you were a little child; because it is the best book that ever was or will be known in the world." ▪

Top: Charles Dickens in his study at Gad's Hill Place.

53 Elizabeth Cady Stanton

As a young girl visiting her father's law office, Elizabeth Cady Stanton was appalled to learn about the laws limiting women's freedom and preventing them from inheriting property.

Born in Jonestown, New York, to a wealthy and politically important family, Elizabeth Cady Stanton studied at the Troy Female Seminary and had the best education then available to women. Her father, Daniel Cady—a lawyer, judge, and United States congressman—told her that these statutes limiting women's freedom could be overturned by appeals to the government. Little did he know then that his daughter would make fighting for women's rights her life's work.

It was through her work as an abolitionist alongside her husband, Henry Stanton, that Elizabeth Stanton met Lucretia Mott. In 1847, inspired by Mott's feminist views, Stanton joined her and three other women to coordinate a women's rights convention in Seneca Falls, New York, setting a precedent for future conventions. Before the 300 attendees, Stanton read her Declaration of Rights and Sentiments, a reworking of the Declaration of Independence that demanded equal rights for women, including the right to vote.

Stanton and her friend Susan B. Anthony became key leaders in the decades-long movement that culminated with the Nineteenth Amendment, which gave women the right to vote in the United States.

No stranger to controversy, Stanton angered people on both sides of the suffrage issue when she penned *The Woman's Bible* in 1895. Stanton believed the Bible was a source of the oppression of women, writing in the introduction to *The Woman's' Bible*, "From the inauguration of the movement for woman's emancipation the Bible has been used to hold her in the 'divinely ordained sphere,' prescribed in the Old and New Testaments." Stanton organized a committee of women to contribute to a new Bible commentary on the biblical passages about women, challenging male interpretations of the Bible that they believed were biased against women.

The Woman's Bible ignited a firestorm within the National Woman Suffrage Association (NWSA), the organization Stanton and Anthony established together in 1869. Overriding Anthony's objections, the NWSA leadership voted to reject the book and to censure Stanton.

Undaunted, Stanton continued working independently and with Anthony on behalf of women's rights until her death in 1902—eighteen years before the Nineteenth Amendment became a reality. ∎

Left: Elizabeth Cady Stanton. Portrait ca. 1890.
Right: Women's Suffrage hikers who took part in the walk from New York City to Washington, D.C. to join the National American Woman Suffrage Association parade of March 3, 1913.

54 Frederick Douglass

Frederick Douglas put a face, a name, and an eloquent voice on the institution of slavery in pre–Civil War America.

During a Fourth of July speech he gave in Rochester, New York, in 1852, Douglass invokes the Bible in an impassioned argument against slavery. He said, "This Fourth of July is yours, not mine. You may rejoice, I must mourn." He went on to quote the Bible's Psalm 137:1, "By the waters of Babylon, there we sat down and wept, when we remembered Zion," and he referred to his task as a former slave to "sing the Lord's song in a foreign land" (Psalm 137:4).

Born as a slave in Maryland to a black mother and a white father presumed to be the plantation master, Douglass escaped to the North at the age of twenty. He renamed himself "Douglass" after the hero of *The Lady of the Lake* by Sir Walter Scott.

In the 1840s, Douglass participated in the abolitionist movement and wrote his first autobiography, *Life and Times of Frederick Douglass,* in 1845. For sixteen years,

he edited a newspaper. Through his editorials and speeches, including speaking engagements in Europe, he made a powerful indictment against slavery.

Douglass served as President Abraham Lincoln's adviser, and he helped to recruit northern blacks for the Union Army. In 1889, President Benjamin Harrison appointed Douglass as the US Minister to the Republic of Haiti.

Douglass included biblical allusions and metaphors in his speeches. For example, he used Acts 17:26, "He made from one man every nation of mankind to live on all the face of the earth," to teach that all men should be equal since God made all human beings from one man.

In his three autobiographies, Douglass recalled that, as a slave, he desperately wanted to learn to read so that he could read the Bible. Because the United States maintained slavery throughout much of his lifetime, Douglass held that the Bible, not any church or political organization, was the ultimate authority. "Between the Christianity of this land and the Christianity of Christ, I recognize the widest possible difference," he wrote. ∎

Eng⁴ by A.H.Ritchie

Top: Slavery in Africa. The Treaty, vintage engraved illustration. Journal des Voyage, Travel Journal, (1880-81).
Left: Frederick Douglass (ca 1817-1895)

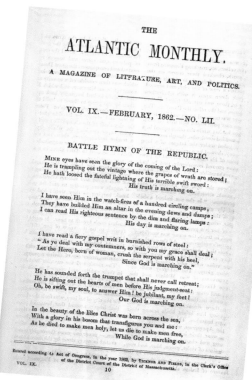

55 Julia Ward Howe

If America were to adopt another song as its national anthem, a frontrunner would be "The Battle Hymn of the Republic." The song, with lyrics written in 1861 by Julia Ward Howe, has become an American classic—inspiring soldiers, suffragists, civil rights leaders, and novelists.

Howe wrote the lyrics as a poem while visiting a Union army camp near Washington, DC, in 1861. She sent her poem to the *Atlantic Monthly*, where it was published in February 1862. Her payment was five dollars. She received no byline.

Women's rights leaders created an adapted version of the song in 1890 with their "Battle Hymn of the Suffragists." In 1915, union organizers paid homage to the "Battle Hymn" with their own "Solidarity Forever." John Steinbeck's Pulitzer Prize–winning novel, *The Grapes of Wrath,* got its title from the song, and its lyrics appeared on the front page of his book.

The day before he was killed, Martin Luther King Jr. spoke before sanitation workers on strike in Memphis, Tennessee. "I want you to know tonight that we, as a people, will get to the Promised Land," King said. He closed his speech with the opening line of Howe's anthem: "Mine eyes have seen the glory of the coming of the Lord."

The song was featured at the September 11 memorial service held at the National Cathedral in Washington, DC. In a 2010 tribute to the song published in the *Atlantic Monthly,* writer Dominic Tierney called it "a warrior's cry and a call to arms. Its vivid portrait of sacred violence captures how Americans fight wars, from the minié balls of the Civil War to the shock and awe of Iraq."

Howe was raised as a Protestant, and she made many references to the Bible in "The Battle Hymn of the Republic," including Isaiah 6:5, Revelation 14 and 15, and passages from Psalms, Job, Joel, and Ezekiel.

Indeed, throughout the nation's history, Howe's lyrics have celebrated American culture in churches, at patriotic celebrations, and at times of mourning. ■

Top: Julia Ward Howe author of the 'Battle Hymn of the Republic', ca. 1906.
Top left: Battle Hymn of the Republic

56 Florence Nightingale

Florence Nightingale was a familiar and welcome figure to her patients as she tended them at night by the light of the lantern she carried. Lovingly nicknamed "the Lady with the Lamp," Nightingale was a pioneer in the nursing profession.

Named for her birthplace, Florence, Italy, Nightingale was raised in a wealthy and prominent British family. She received a classical education, including studies in mathematics along with German, French, and Italian. From a young age, she became active in serving the poor people neighboring her family's estate.

However, when she talked with her parents about her desire to become a nurse, they forbade her to pursue the plan. At that time, nursing was viewed as menial labor for someone of the Nightingale social status, and her parents expected her to marry a man of means.

In 1850, determined to follow her passion, Nightingale enrolled at the Institution of Protestant Deaconesses in Kaiserswerth, Germany, as a nursing student. She eventually moved to London, where she took a nursing position at a hospital for ailing governesses and volunteered at another hospital.

When the Crimean War broke out, there was a great need for nurses to help injured British soldiers. The work of Nightingale and her team of nurses greatly improved unsanitary conditions at the field hospitals of Crimea and, according to some reports, reduced their death rate by two-thirds. In addition to "the Lady with the Lamp," some soldiers called Nightingale "the Angel of the Crimea."

Nightingale often said she had been called directly by God to "service." She revealed her understanding of the Bible in a letter to her father: "It strikes me that all truth lies between these two: man saying to God, as Samuel did, Lord, here am I, and God saying to man as Christ did, in the storm, lo it is I, be not afraid. And neither is complete, without the other."

When she was in her thirties, Nightingale wrote *Suggestions for Thought to the Searchers after Truth among the Artizans*, an 829-page work offering her spiritual thoughts to the working classes of England.

In 1860, Nightingale founded Saint Thomas' Hospital and the Nightingale Training School for Nurses. Inspired by Mary's words recorded in Luke 1:38, Nightingale once told a night nurse, "May we all answer the angel as Mary did: 'Behold the handmaid of the Lord: be it unto me according to Thy word.'" ∎

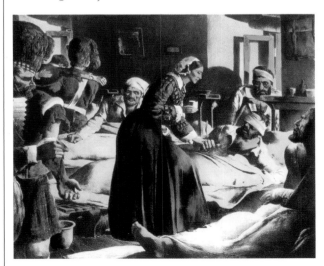

Left: Florence Nightingale (1820-1910), photograph ca. 1880
Bottom: Florence Nightingale 1820-1910 ministering to soldiers at Scutari, a suburb of Istanbul, during the Crimean War, Lithograph by Robert Riggs ca. 1930 with modern watercolor.

57 Harriet Tubman

Harriet Tubman was often called "Moses" because she guided so many people to freedom from slavery. The nickname held special meaning for Tubman since she found inspiration as a child from the Bible stories her mother told her about Moses delivering the Israelites from bondage.

Raised as a slave in eastern Maryland, Harriet Tubman escaped to the North in 1849. She then risked her own freedom nineteen times as she returned to the South to help some 300 other slaves escape. As a result, she became one of the most successful conductors on the Underground Railroad. "I never lost a passenger," she later said.

Using her motto, "I can't die but once," Tubman eluded frustrated slave catchers who were eager to win the astounding sum of $40,000 that was offered for her capture. She told friends and fellow abolitionists that her strength came from God.

"I always tole God," she said, 'I'm gwine to hole stiddy on you, an' you've got to see me through.'"

During the Civil War, Tubman worked as a spy and a scout for the Union Army and as a recruiter of slaves for the troops. When she was well into her eighties, she actively campaigned for the women's suffrage movement.

Before she died, Tubman turned to the Bible for strength, as she had so many times during her life. She quoted the words of Jesus recorded in John 14:3 ("I go and prepare a place for you") to the friends and family gathered by her bedside. Tubman was buried with military honors in Fort Hill Cemetery in Auburn, New York. ▪

Close-up of the Harriet Tubman statue in Boston's South End neighborhood.

58 Josephine Butler

Josephine Butler used tragedy from her own life to help others. She was instrumental in social reforms in nineteenth-century Britain, including bringing awareness to the plight of prostitutes and working women.

When her six-year-old daughter died after falling from a balcony, Butler's grief motivated her to act. "[I] became possessed with an irresistible urge to go forth and find some pain keener than my own, to meet with people more unhappy than myself," she wrote.

Born in 1828 into an upper-middle-class family in Northumberland, England, Butler grew up with abolitionist parents who educated her in political activism. She was a student of the Bible, reading Scripture regularly and carefully, paying special attention to the biblical teachings about the plight of the outcast.

When Butler and her husband moved to Liverpool, she encountered poor women who had turned to prostitution in order to feed their children. Butler also discovered servant girls who, after being sexually exploited by their employers, were left destitute when they became pregnant.

"The degradation of these poor unhappy women is not degradation for them alone; it is a blow to the dignity of every virtuous woman too," she wrote. "It is dishonor done to me, it is the shaming of every woman in every country of the world."

Butler worked to repeal the Contagious Diseases Act, which allowed police to arrest and forcibly inspect women they suspected of being prostitutes. She also helped to expose child prostitution and child sex trafficking between Belgium and Britain.

Butler was often heckled and threatened for her work, and her husband almost lost his job. The couple relied upon their faith and their knowledge of the Bible for strength. Butler also saw the plight of women, through a biblical lens, describing women "continually dragged and driven to the fashionable markets of lust, and there slain like sheep appointed for slaughter." She also found inspiration in the prophetic narratives in the Bible, believing that she was a "voice crying in the wilderness."

"I felt very weak and lonely," she admitted later. "But there was One who stood by me."

Passionate about her faith, Josephine often said, "God and one woman make a majority." ◼

Josephine Butler, artist unknown

59 Leo Tolstoy

Critics and other authors have hailed Leo Tolstoy as one of history's most authentic and realistic writers about war. Set against the backdrop of the Napoleonic Wars, Tolstoy's *War and Peace*, first published in 1869, includes battle scenes so accurate and detailed that one former general said the book should be required reading for all Russian army officers.

However, Tolstoy was a pacifist whose interpretation of the Sermon on the Mount had a large influence on the nonviolent movement of the twentieth century, including influencing key leaders, Mahatma Gandhi and Martin Luther King Jr.

Tolstoy earned literary acclaim as a young man with his autobiographical works, *Childhood, Boyhood, and Youth* and *Sevastopol Sketches*. He went on to write short stories, novellas, essays, and plays. His novel *Anna Karenina* was voted the "greatest book ever written" in a 2007 *Time* magazine poll.

After the publication of *Anna Karenina*, however, Tolstoy experienced a moral crisis. Increasingly troubled by his aristocratic upbringing and his own wealth, Tolstoy came to believe that the teachings of organized religion contradicted what Jesus taught in the Bible.

Rejecting the authority of the church and the government, he believed in the gospel of the Bible but viewed Jesus of Nazareth as a mere man. He outlined his philosophy in his book *The Kingdom of God Is Within You*, which was published in 1894 and whose title quotes the Gospel of Luke. The literary genius who had written exquisitely about the search for life's meaning seemed to have finally found his.

In 1885, he wrote in his treatise, *My Religion*, "I believe in the doctrine of Jesus, and this is my religion: I believe that nothing but the fulfillment of the doctrine of Jesus can give true happiness to men." ∎

Leo Tolstoy, a portrait of Nicholas Kramskoy, 1873, from the collection of the State Tretyakov Gallery, Moscow.

60 Catherine Booth

At a time when most people thought a woman's place was in the home, Catherine Booth forged new territory as an evangelist and as a theologian.

Born in Ashbourne, United Kingdom, Booth suffered from curvature of the spine as a teenager and often had to spend months at a time resting in bed. She used this time to read the Bible. She also became intrigued by the writings of Charles Finney and John Wesley.

When confronted with the philosophy that women did not belong in ministry, Booth claimed the Bible as her authority, saying, "I would not yield to any man or woman in my love for this Bible. I love this Word and regard it as the standard of all faith and practice."

Booth found a kindred spirit in her husband, William, a minister who traded the pulpit for London's streets. Working together, the Booths developed an organization that was originally called the Christian Mission, which we know today as the Salvation Army. Booth's unofficial title was "Army Mother," and the Salvation Army welcomed women as preachers and in other leadership roles throughout the organization.

Their ministry, which served alcoholics, prostitutes, and criminals, drew complaints from some Christians who felt the "Salvationists" were straying too far from appropriate church decorum.

In defense, Booth again cited the Bible as her guide. The church, she argued, "has made a grand mistake, the same old mistake which we are so prone

to fall into, of exalting the traditions of the elders into the same importance as the Word of God, as the clearly laid down principles of the New Testament."

Booth wrote several books, including *Practical Religion*, *Popular Christianity*, and *Aggressive Christianity*. After her death in 1890, a magazine described her as "the most famous and influential Christian woman of the generation." ∎

Top: Catherine Booth, the mother of the Salvation Army
Left: Salvation Army in London, wood engraving, published in 1883

61 Amanda Berry Smith

Known as "the Singing Pilgrim," Amanda Berry Smith was as an evangelist in India and Africa and a strong advocate for homeless African American children in the United States. While these accomplishments are admirable for anyone, they are particularly so considering Smith was born into a life of slavery in Maryland.

Unlike many slaves, Smith learned to read and write at an early age, and in her autobiography, she notes that her father frequently read to her family from the Bible. Her father also worked to buy her family's freedom, and they were able to move to Pennsylvania. It was during a Methodist worship service in Pennsylvania that Smith recalled she "felt the first faint stirrings of belief" and decided to put her Bible background and her experiences to use to help others.

She began working as a traveling preacher, an unusual occupation for any woman in the nineteenth century but certainly for an African American woman. She encountered racism wherever she went, but she continued preaching from the Bible, often singing for her listeners. She once told someone who challenged her authority to speak to white people, "But I belong to Royalty. I am well acquainted with the King of Kings. I am better known and better understood among the great family above than I am on earth."

Smith eventually traveled to England, where she drew large crowds who were curious to hear her speak, since she was considered a novelty. In 1879, she traveled to India and then she later went to Africa.

Back in the United States, she became a proponent of the temperance movement and spoke on the subject at the Lafayette Avenue Presbyterian Church in Brooklyn, New York, which at the time was the largest church in that denomination.

Smith established the Amanda Smith Orphanage and Industrial Home for Abandoned and Destitute Colored Children in Chicago in 1899. She traveled throughout the country to preach from the Bible and raise money for her work until her death in 1915. ∎

Top: Amanda Berry Smith, c1899, by Norman Barton Wood

Lottie Moon

Born in Virginia into a Baptist family that valued education for both boys and girls, Lottie Moon was one of the first women to earn a master's degree at a southern university. She began a teaching career but decided to join her younger sister, Edmonia, who was the first single woman to travel to China as a Baptist missionary in 1871. Moon ended up spending nearly forty years living and working in China as a missionary.

As she sought to gather support for her work in China, Moon often referenced the Bible. In a letter for a Southern Baptist missions journal in 1888, she wrote that she and another female worker needed assistance: "As I saw her last week instructing patiently for hours the men who eagerly gathered around her, my memory was haunted by the words of Scripture: 'That no man take thy crown.' It seemed to me that here was a woman doing the work of some young man among Southern Baptists in America who ought to be here, and that when the harvest should be garnered in Heaven and the laborers receive their reward, the Master would place on her head the crown that should have been his!"

Moon urged Southern Baptists to prioritize missions. She helped establish the Women's Missionary Union, and in 1888 it began collecting an annual Christmastime offering. The Lottie Moon Christmas Offering for Missions continues today and has collected nearly $2 billion since 1888.

Although she was only four feet three inches tall, Charlotte "Lottie" Moon had a big impact on international missions.

In her article "Why Many Missionaries Are Needed," Moon explained the importance of both volunteers and funding. After a positive response to the gospel message, she wrote, "What these people need—next to the grace of God in their hearts—is to see the life of Jesus Christ set before them in the concrete, in the holy life of the missionary."

Top: Lottie Moon, Women's Missionary Union Pamphlet ND
Bottom: A Southern Baptist Church in rural surroundings

63 Woodrow Wilson

Although he had pledged to keep the United States out of the war, Woodrow Wilson led the nation into World War I in 1917 after Germany announced it would be targeting "all sea traffic."

Telling Congress that "armed neutrality, it now appears, is impracticable," President Wilson expressed "a profound sense of the solemn and even tragical character of the step I am taking, and of the grave responsibilities which it involves."

As the twenty-eighth president of the United States, Wilson served two terms from 1913 to 1919. He previously served as governor of New Jersey and as president of Princeton University.

In addition to leading the nation into and out of the Great War, Wilson helped negotiate the Treaty of Versailles in 1919. Although most of his "Fourteen Points" advocating for human and democratic rights were not included in the final treaty, his idea for a League of Nations to ensure a lasting peace was adopted. Wilson's idea of a "covenant amongst nations" has a Biblical echo.

During his presidency, Wilson created the Federal Reserve and supported the Nineteenth Amendment, which gave women the right to vote.

The son of a Presbyterian minister from Augusta, Georgia, Wilson read the Bible and attended church all his life. He spoke directly about the influence of the Bible on America when he remarked, "The Bible (with its individual value of the human soul) is undoubtedly the

book that has made democracy and been the source of all progress."

Referring to the Bible often in his speeches, Wilson commented, "America is not ahead of the other nations of the world because she is rich. Nothing makes America great except her thoughts, except her ideals, except her acceptance of those standards of judgment which are written large upon these pages of revelation."

Wilson suffered a severe stroke in 1919 during his second term in office, and he died in 1924. Many historians believe Wilson was incapacitated by the stroke and that his wife, Edith, conducted his duties as president during his long illness. The former First Lady denied the allegations until her death in 1961. ■

Top: President Woodrow Wilson (1856-1924) in 1919 portrait.
Left: Early 1900 postcard depicting Yankee soldiers going into action in France during WWI

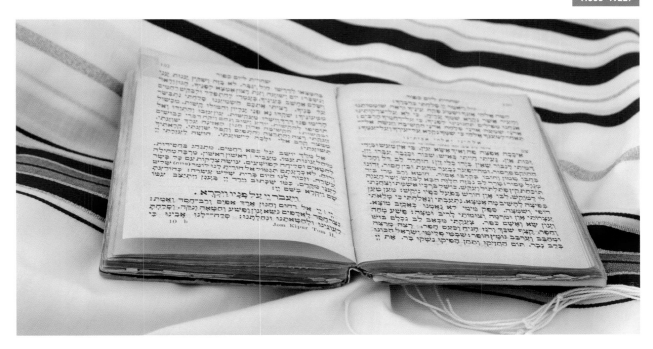

64 Eliezer Ben-Yehuda

Before the State of Israel was reestablished in 1948, the Hebrew language was only used during religious ceremonies. In fact, it was considered a "dead language" even though the Hebrew Bible was originally written in Hebrew. But Eliezer Ben-Yehuda wanted to bring the language of his people and the Bible back to life.

Ben-Yehuda was born in Lithuania in 1858; "he was a prodigy, so at the age of three he was reading Hebrew in the Scriptures and prayer books." He fell in love with the language and was determined to resurrect it as a modern language rather than reserve it only for Jewish religious ceremonies. During his study of the tongue, he discovered that Hebrew needed some adjustments in order to be relevant as a modern language, so he invented necessary words to complete it.

Ultimately, Ben-Yehuda is credited with reviving the biblical language and making it a modern language once again when he published the seventeen-volume *A Complete Dictionary of Ancient and Modern Hebrew.* As a result, Israel recognizes Hebrew as one of its official languages today. Jewish historian Cecil Roth reflects: "Before Ben-Yehuda . . . Jews could speak Hebrew; after him they did." ■

Top: Prayer Shawl - Tallit, Jewish religious symbol.
Bottom: Eliezer Ben-Yehuda. 1858-1922, taken in 1905, Widener Library, Cambridge, Massachusetts

65 Mahatma Gandhi

"Strength does not come from physical capacity. It comes from an indomitable will."

When Mahatma Gandhi spoke these lines, he was probably referring to his native India and its struggle for independence from the strong British Empire. But he could just as easily have been talking about himself.

Standing at a mere five feet four inches and with a slim build, Gandhi's appearance belied his inner strength. His methods of nonviolent civil disobedience not only helped him lead his country to freedom but also inspired other world leaders, including Nelson Mandela and Martin Luther King Jr.

As an Indian immigrant living and working as a lawyer in South Africa, Mahatma Gandhi experienced racial discrimination beginning at the age of twenty-four. When he refused to give up his seat on a train to a European passenger, Gandhi was beaten and kicked off the train by the white driver. That incident was the catalyst for his philosophy of passive resistance and for his life's work as an activist for social change.

Gandhi returned to India in 1915, where he led the Indian Independence Movement and initiated several significant campaigns, including the Salt March and Quit India. The Salt March was a protest against the British Salt Act of 1882, which imposed a stiff tax on salt and prohibited Indians from collecting or selling it. Thousands of Indians joined Gandhi in a 24-day, 241-mile march to Dandi, where they could produce salt from seawater. As a result, 80,000 Indians were jailed, and the world took notice.

The 1942 Quit India campaign he spearheaded eventually resulted in the end of British rule over India. Gandhi also sought to help his people by campaigning for women's rights and by working to improve the lives of India's "Untouchables."

Although Gandhi was a Hindu, in a speech in 1925, Gandhi referred to his study of the Bible. He said, "Although I am myself not a Christian, as a humble student of the Bible, who approaches it with faith and reverence, I wish respectfully to place before you the essence of the Sermon on the Mount. . . . There are thousands of men and women today who, though they may not have heard about the Bible or Jesus, have more faith and are more god-fearing than Christians who know the Bible and who talk of its Ten Commandments."

India honors Mahatma Gandhi as the Father of the Nation and celebrates his birthday, October 2, as a national holiday. Throughout the world, that day also is recognized as International Day of Non-Violence. ■

Top: The bronze statue of Mahatma Gandhi in London, Parliament Square. The sculptor: Philip Jackson.

66 Winston Churchill

"We shall defend our island, whatever the cost may be, we shall fight on the beaches, we shall fight on the landing grounds, we shall fight in the fields and in the streets, we shall fight in the hills; we shall never surrender."

With these stirring words uttered before Britain's House of Commons on June 4, 1940, not long after the evacuation from Dunkirk, Winston Churchill led his nation through the perils of World War II.

Born in Blenheim Palace, England, into a life of wealth and privilege, Winston Churchill dedicated his life to public service and is arguably England's best-known and best-loved statesman.

After a childhood marked by little parental affection and a poor academic record, Churchill found his calling in the British military in 1895 and served around the world in Cuba, India, Spain, and South Africa.

As a military hero, Churchill entered politics in 1900 and then served as the head of the British Navy in World War I. Criticized for strategic errors he made during the war, Churchill began serving in the House of Commons and turned to writing and lecturing. When he identified the growing threat of Adolph Hitler and his Nazi regime in 1933, Churchill was initially dismissed as a warmonger.

Appointed prime minister on the same day Hitler invaded France and Belgium, Churchill's strength of character and his fiery rhetoric helped lead the Allies to victory over Nazi Germany in 1945.

Throughout his career, Churchill declared his admiration for the Judeo-Christian ethical code, which he said was "incomparably the most precious possession of mankind, worth in fact the fruits of all other wisdom and learning put together."

In a 1931 article for the *Sunday Chronicle,* he wrote, "We believe that the most scientific view, the most up-to-date and rationalistic conception, will find its fullest satisfaction in taking the Bible story literally, and in identifying one of the greatest human beings with the most decisive leap forward ever discernible in the human story." ▪

Left: A stamp printed in Canada shows Sir Winston Churchill (1874-1965), portrait photograph by Yousuf Karsh, 1941
Bottom: The Palace of Westminster is the meeting place of the House of Commons and the House of Lords, the two houses of the Parliament of the United Kingdom.

67 Konrad Adenauer

Imprisoned in 1934 for his anti-Nazi stance and arrested in 1944 for his alleged involvement in a plot to kill Adolph Hitler, Konrad Adenauer went on to play a leading role in rebuilding Germany after World War II. He served as chancellor from 1949 to 1963.

A native of Cologne, Adenauer studied at the Freiburg, Munich, and Bonn universities before he became a lawyer like his father before him. He began his political career as a member of the Cologne City Council, and in 1917, he was elected lord mayor of the city. Three years later, he was elected to the Provincial Diet (formal assembly). When he became president of the Prussian State Council in 1920, he was one of the most influential politicians in Germany.

In 1933 when the Nazis rose to power, Adenauer was removed from his offices, and throughout the Nazi period, he was persecuted by the Gestapo. In 1944, after the failed assassination plot against Hitler, he was imprisoned a second time but was released prior to the end of the war because of illness.

After the war, American peacekeeping forces appointed Adenauer the mayor of Cologne, and he formed the Christian Democratic Union (CDU), the party that would eventually elect him chancellor.

Adenauer was also instrumental in the formation of NATO and in Germany's contribution to the European Economic Community, which would later be succeeded by the European Union.

Raised as a Catholic, Adenauer believed that the only way to revive Germany was for it to return to its Christian roots. Alluding to the Bible's Great Commandment, recorded in Matthew 22:39 and Mark 12:31, which admonishes people to "love your neighbor as yourself," Adenauer wrote, "One of the fundamental principles of Christianity is the love of neighbor, respect for our neighbors." "That principle does not apply only to individuals; it applies also to the attitudes of nations toward other nations."

"Western Christianity denies the dominance of the state, and insists on the dignity and liberty of the individual," he continued. "Only this traditional Christian principle could now help us to show the German people a new political goal, to recall them to a new political life. This conviction would give our party the strength to raise Germany from the depths." ∎

Top: Coins of Germany. German statesman Konrad Adenauer and the German eagle depicted in old Deutsche Mark coins.

68 Albert Einstein

Although he was the mathematical and scientific genius who gave the world the theory of relativity, Albert Einstein believed the problem of the existence of God to be "too vast for our limited minds."

"My religiosity consists in a humble admiration of the infinitely superior spirit that reveals itself in the little that we, with our weak and transitory understanding, can comprehend of reality," Einstein wrote. "Morality is of the highest importance—but for us, not for God."

This brilliant German scientist is considered the most influential physicist of the twentieth century and perhaps of all time. In 1921, Albert received the Nobel Prize in Physics for his findings about packets of light (quanta) and other groundbreaking research about the way the universe works. Targeted by the Nazis during the 1930s, Einstein immigrated to the United States. His research—in particular his equation $E=MC^2$, which states that energy and mass are interchangeable—led to the development of the atomic bomb and atomic power.

Though Jewish by heritage and raised by parents who were Ashkenazi Jews, Albert Einstein attended a Catholic public elementary school and then a public high school. That education exposed him to the Bible at an early age.

When asked about the existence of Jesus, he replied, "No one can read the Gospels without feeling the actual presence of Jesus. His personality pulsates in every word. No myth is filled with such life. How different, for instance, is the impression which we receive from an account of legendary heroes of antiquity like Theseus. Theseus and other heroes of his type lack the authentic vitality of Jesus."

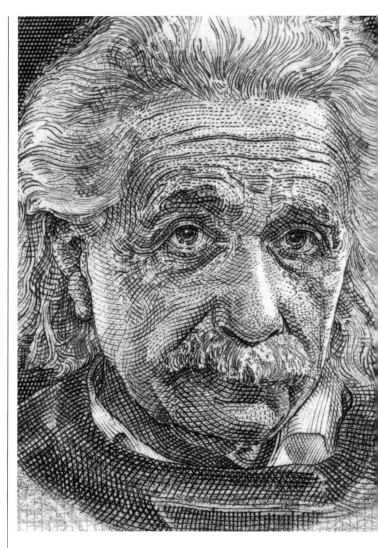

Einstein was also familiar with the Bible's book of Psalms, explaining, "The Jewish tradition also contains something else, something which finds splendid expression in many of the Psalms, namely, a sort of intoxicated joy and amazement at the beauty and grandeur of this world, of which man can form just a faint notion." ∎

Top: Albert Einstein (1879-1955) on a 5-Pound
1968 banknote from Israel
Left: Theory of relativity by Albert Einstein

69 Cecil B. DeMille

For the filming of his 1923 silent epic, The Ten Commandments, Cecil B. DeMille set out to recreate Ancient Egypt on ten acres of sand dunes located 175 miles north of Hollywood.

He hired more than 1,000 craftsmen to build the main set, which included four 20-ton statues of Ramses II, 21 huge sphinxes, 300 chariots, and a 110-foot temple wall. He then added 3,000 animals and 2,500 extra actors for more realism. When he finished shooting the film, DeMille demanded that the entire set be demolished and covered in sand to prevent any other director from using it.

By the early 1920s, DeMille was already known for his extravagance, but the filmmaker's lavish behavior netted box office gold. Between 1913 and 1956, DeMille made seventy silent and sound films, such as *Cleopatra* (1934), *The Greatest Show on Earth* (1952), and *Union Pacific* (1939).

Many of his most popular films were based on the Bible, including *Samson and Delilah* (1949), *The King of Kings* (1927), and the 1956 remake of *The Ten Commandments*, for which he flew the cast and crew to Egypt.

Raised as an Episcopalian, Cecil DeMille took the adaptation of the Bible seriously. Before he started filming *The Ten Commandments*, for example, DeMille reportedly gave a Bible to every studio employee along with a personal note that read: "As I intend to film practically the entire book of Exodus, the Bible should never be away from you."

The filmmaker consulted rabbis, pastors, and other church advisers to ensure that his films were biblically accurate. He also was a Hollywood showman, however. While preparing for his film about the life of Christ, *The King of Kings*, he justified the addition of a love affair between Mary Magdalene and Judas Iscariot with this comment to a church adviser: "It is not possible to produce a great and successful film dealing with historic characters and not have a love-interest."

Known as a founder of the motion-picture industry, DeMille paved the way for an onslaught of Hollywood movies based on the Bible. DeMille was a student of the Bible all his life. He read from it with his children each night and during his lunch break each day. He once stated, "My ministry has been to make religious movies and to get more people to read the Bible than anyone else ever has." ▪

Top: Cecil B. DeMille shooting *The Ten Commandments* in 1956
Bottom: Cecil B. De Mille star on the Hollywood Walk of Fame in Hollywood, California

70 David Ben-Gurion

during the Arab–Israeli War in 1948, Jewish militias united into the Israel Defense Forces (IDF).

Describing himself as neither an Orthodox Jew nor a Reformed Jew, Ben-Gurion studied the Bible throughout his life. Ben-Gurion considered the Tanakh (the Hebrew Bible, sometimes called the Old Testament) as the most important book not only for Jews but for all people because of its teachings on the equality of all nations, human values, law and justice, universal camaraderie, the pursuit of peace, and compassion and truth.

After leaving politics in 1970, Ben-Gurion spent his retirement in a modest home on the kibbutz. He wrote extensively about Israel's history, including his book *Israel: A Personal History*, which was published in 1971.

Under the glass on his desk, Ben-Gurion kept this quote, adapted from Isaiah 45:18: "Thus said God creator of the heaven; He is God who formed the earth and all that it produces, He fashioned it." ∎

"We hereby proclaim the establishment of the Jewish state in Palestine, to be called Israel."

With that simple declaration on May 14, 1948, at the Tel Aviv Art Museum, David Ben-Gurion made history. The crowd applauded and wept as Ben-Gurion established the first Jewish state in 2,000 years and stepped into his role as its first prime minister.

Born in Płońsk, Russian Empire (now Poland), David Ben-Gurion was educated in a Hebrew school founded by his father, a fervent Zionist. After graduation, he taught in a Jewish school in Warsaw, where he joined Poalei Zion (Workers of Zion) and championed the movement to establish a Jewish homeland.

Revered as Israel's founding father, Ben-Gurion helped write the Israeli Declaration of Independence, and he was first to sign the document. Under his leadership

Left: David Ben Gurion (1886-1973) on a 50 Sheqalim 1978 banknote from Israel
Right: Israel flag

71 Faye Edgerton

The Navajo Indians called Faye Edgerton "The One Who Understands."

It is easy to understand why. Edgerton worked for nearly fifty years learning the Navajo language and working on a Bible translation for the Navajo people.

Born in Nebraska as the daughter of a Presbyterian elder, Faye Edgerton was a normal American teenager, going to school, attending church, and enjoying activities with her friends. Two years after her high school graduation, however, a bout with scarlet fever left her completely deaf for several weeks.

When her hearing remarkably returned, Edgerton was a changed person with different priorities. She enrolled in Moody Bible Institute in Chicago and committed her life to missionary service.

She spent four years teaching the Bible in Korea until illness forced her to return to the United States, where the Presbyterian board reassigned her to a Navajo reservation. At that time, the Navajo language was labeled "inhibitive" and Bible teaching was done in English.

However, Edgerton's teaching experiences in Korea had taught her that the faith of Korean Christians was strong because they had the Bible in their own language. She decided to study the Navajo language on her own.

In 1944, Edgerton joined Wycliffe Bible Translators, where she worked with a team to draft the first complete version of a Navajo New Testament. One of her assistants, a Navajo man named Roger, had taught himself to read his native tongue from an English–Navajo dictionary. "This is not just a missionary talking to us in another language—this is God's word in Navajo," Roger said of the Bible translation. "It is just like God talking!"

When the completed translation was published in 1956, it was a huge success. It spurred the Navajo people to learn to read and write in their own tongue. Edgerton, who was then in her sixties, next began learning Apache, and after nine years of work, the Apache New Testament was also published.

Edgerton kept studying and working on Native American translations of the Bible until shortly before her death in 1968. ▪

United States, Arizona, Monument Valley
Navajo Tribal Park

72 Dwight Eisenhower

As the Supreme Allied Commander in charge of D-Day in World War II, Dwight D. Eisenhower earned his place as an American hero.

"I am the most intensely religious man I know," Eisenhower stated after returning home from World War II. "Nobody goes through six years of war without faith. That doesn't mean that I adhere to any sect. A democracy cannot exist without a religious base."

Raised in Abilene, Kansas, by parents who were active in the Brethren in Christ Church, Dwight Eisenhower was familiar with the Bible but not a member of a church when he moved into the White House in 1953.

However, he wrote and read his own prayer at his inaugural, and he joined the Presbyterian Church just weeks later. He also became the first and only president to date to be baptized while in office.

Though some US presidents have taken their oaths of office with the Bible closed, others have had the book open to specific passages with special meaning. For both ceremonies, Eisenhower chose Psalm 33:12 ("Blessed is the nation whose God is the Lord, the people whom he has chosen as his heritage!"). In 1953, he also had a Bible open to 2 Chronicles 7:14 ("If my people who are called by my name humble themselves, and pray and seek my face and turn from their wicked ways, then will I hear from heaven and will forgive their sin and heal their land"). ▪

A bronze statue of Dwight D. Eisenhower in his WWII jacket by Robert L. Dean, Jr.

73 Corrie ten Boom

Corrie ten Boom was born in Amsterdam, the Netherlands. She was a Christian who, along with her father and other family members, saved the lives of nearly 800 Jews during the Holocaust by hiding small groups in their Dutch watchmaking shop until safe passage could be made for their escape.

Betrayed by an informant, the ten Booms were arrested by Nazi authorities and taken to concentration camps. Both Corrie's father and sister died while they were there, but due to a clerical error, Corrie was freed a week before she was scheduled to be killed.

Corrie's amazing story, which she related in her 1971 book, *The Hiding Place* (the title inspired by Psalm 119:114.) does not end there, however. After the war, she returned to the Netherlands to establish a rehabilitation center for survivors of the concentration camp. Then, in 1946, at age fifty-three, she built an international ministry that shared a message of love and forgiveness.

After a speaking engagement in 1947, for example, Corrie recognized a man who was walking toward her. "It came back with a rush: the huge room with its harsh overhead lights, the pathetic pile of dresses and shoes in the center of the floor, the shame of walking naked past this man," she wrote. "I could see my sister's frail form ahead of me, ribs sharp beneath the parchment skin."

The man had been a guard at Ravensbruck concentration camp, where Corrie's sister Betsie had died just three days before Corrie was released. The man did not recognize Corrie, but having heard her speech, he sought her forgiveness.

As she faced the man, Corrie's belief system was tested. Verses from the Bible filled her mind, especially Matthew 6:15: "If you do not forgive others their trespasses, neither will your Father forgive your trespasses."

"And so woodenly, mechanically, I thrust my hand into the one stretched out to me," she wrote. "And as I did, an incredible thing took place. The current started in my shoulder, raced down my arm, sprang into our joined hands. And then this healing warmth seemed to flood my whole being, bringing tears to my eyes." ∎

Top: Captive women working at the Ravensbruck concentration camp in Berlin, Germany
Left: Corrie ten Boom with actress Jeannette Clift, who played Corrie in the 1975 film, *The Hiding Place*

74 J. R. R. Tolkien

J. R. R. Tolkien's accomplishments extended beyond merely writing novels. He created a new world for his readers to explore—a world called Middle Earth, with its own maps and language and populated by talking trees, human-like animals, elves and goblins, and marvelous hairy-footed creatures called hobbits.

Tolkien's book *The Hobbit* (1937) and his trilogy the Lord of the Rings (1954-1955) have captivated readers since their publication and have inspired new fans with the twenty-first-century films based on them. The books rank on most lists of the best-selling books of all time.

John Ronald Reuel Tolkien was born in South Africa. After his father died from complications of rheumatic fever when the author was four, his mother moved him and his younger brother to the English countryside near Birmingham.

After their mother died in 1904, the young brothers were sent to live with relatives and later to boarding homes. Tolkien went on to study at Oxford University, specializing in Anglo-Saxon and Germanic languages and classic literature. In World War I, he fought in the ferocious Battle of the Somme. His battalion suffered devastating losses, and Tolkien subsequently suffered from ongoing health problems that caused him to be released from service.

He later revealed that he used his horrific war memories to create the fictional Battle of Mordor. He recalled that he began writing about Middle Earth "by candle light in bell-tents, even some down in dugouts under shell fire." While recuperating in the hospital in 1917, he created a series of stories that drew on themes from the Bible and involved dwarves, gnomes, and orcs in a great fight for the future of his imaginary realm.

After the war, Tolkien taught English language and literature at both the University of Leeds and Oxford, focusing on Old and Middle English. He produced a translation of *Beowulf* in 1926 and edited an authoritative edition of *Sir Gawain and the Green Knight*.

Tolkien and writer and apologist C. S. Lewis became good friends at Oxford, and Lewis credited Tolkien with his conversion to Christianity. Just after the conclusion of the Second Vatican Council, Tolkien served as an editor of the Jerusalem Bible, which was published in 1966. His chief contribution was the translation of the book of Jonah.

Raised as a Catholic, Tolkien infused his interest in mythology with his love of the Bible. He once commented that the Christian message was a myth like any other, except that it was the one that was true. He also drew upon biblical narratives for inspiration for his own stories. *The Silmarillion*'s account of the creation of Middle-earth has elements of the Genesis description of creation. ■

Top: A photo of J. R. R. Tolkien taken in the 1960s
Bottom: Hobbiton - movie set created for filming the Lord of the Rings and "Hobbit" movies

75 Robert Jackson

Robert Jackson took a temporary leave from his role as a Supreme Court justice to take a position as the chief prosecutor for the United States at the Nuremberg trials of Nazi war criminals. He considered his work there to be the crowning achievement of his legal career.

"Germany became one vast torture chamber," Jackson said in his opening statement at the trials on November 21, 1945. "Cries of its victims were heard round the world and brought shudders to civilized people everywhere. I am one who received during this war most atrocity tales with suspicion and skepticism. But the proof here will be so overwhelming that I venture to predict not one word I have spoken will be denied. These defendants will only deny personal responsibility or knowledge."

Born in Spring Creek, Pennsylvania, Robert Jackson moved to Frewsburg, New York, as a child. After attending Albany Law School, he served as an attorney in New York State and was later appointed as general counsel to the IRS by President Franklin D. Roosevelt. He went on to serve as US Attorney General until Roosevelt nominated him to the Supreme Court in 1941.

Following World War II, some of the Allied Nations were in favor of executing war criminals or conducting brief court martials to determine their punishment. Jackson, however, was outspoken in his support of a fair trial to decide their guilt or innocence. Roosevelt's successor, President Harry S. Truman, appointed Jackson as chief counsel for the Nuremberg Trials, which tried such infamous Nazis as Hermann Goring and Rudolf Hess.

Jackson based his understanding of the importance of a fair trial on a biblical foundation, including Deuteronomy 19:15, which states, "A single witness shall not suffice against a person for any crime or for any wrong in connection with any offense that he has committed."

In a speech he gave at the National Cathedral in Washington, DC, Jackson said of the Bible:

"In its judicial functions, it was in many ways far in advance of its time, especially in protection of the accused. . . . Two witnesses were required to convict, hearsay was rejected, and circumstantial evidence was not admitted. An accused could testify but could not be made to incriminate himself, and a confession, unless corroborated, was not sufficient to convict."

The Nuremberg Trials set a precedent that individuals must be held personally accountable for their involvement in war crimes. ■

Left: Robert H. Jackson - US Supreme Court Justice and chief prosecutor at the Nuremberg trials
Top: The courthouse in Nuremberg, where the Nuremberg trials took place

76 Dorothy Day

In a historic address before Congress in 2015, Pope Francis named Dorothy Day in his short list of "four great Americans," which included Abraham Lincoln, Thomas Merton, and Martin Luther King Jr. The pope said Day helped to build a better future for America and to shape fundamental American values.

In honoring Day, Pope Francis commented on "her social activism, her passion for justice and for the cause of the oppressed, [which] were inspired by the Gospel, her faith, and the example of the saints."

Born in Brooklyn Heights, New York, eight-year-old Dorothy Day was reading the Bible with her sister, Della, when she had her first significant religious experience. "I remember we were in the attic," Day writes. "I was sitting behind a table, pretending I was the teacher, reading aloud from a Bible that I had found. Slowly, as I read, a new personality impressed itself on me. I was being introduced to someone and I knew almost immediately that I was discovering God."

Day recalled that the love and joy she experienced after the birth of her daughter, Tamar, in 1926 helped lead her to God. Her position on nonviolence and passivism then grew out of her commitment to follow Jesus. She quoted the apostle Peter from Acts 5:29, "We ought to obey God rather than men" (KJV).

In 1933, she cofounded the Catholic Worker movement, an organization still active today, which is committed to nonviolent protests against injustice, war, racism, and violence of all forms. She played an active role in social justice issues in the 1960s. ∎

Top: A photo of Dorothy Day taken in 1916

77 C.S. Lewis

Best known as the author of the allegorical Chronicles of Narnia books for children, C. S. Lewis was an outspoken atheist as a young man.

His honest explorations of his own conversion to Christianity and the challenges that tragedy brought to his faith inspired his contemporary readers and the listeners of his World War II–era radio broadcasts. His writings continue to influence people today.

Born in Ireland in 1898, Lewis served as a professor at Oxford and later Cambridge University, dedicating most of his life to studying and teaching. Known by the nickname "Jack," Lewis grew up in a home where education was highly valued.

"There were books in the study, books in the dining room, books in the cloakroom, books (two deep) in the great bookcase on the landing, books in a bedroom, books piled as high as my shoulder in the cistern attic, books of all kinds," Lewis recalled, and he spent much of his youth reading. After his only brother, Warren, went to English boarding school in 1905, Lewis said he retreated into an imaginary world of knights in armor and of animals dressed as people. He also began to write and illustrate his own stories.

When his beloved mother died from cancer three months before his tenth birthday, Lewis not only suffered his own grief, but he was affected by the fact that his father never recovered from the tragedy. Lewis moved away from the Bible teaching of his mother, a distance that increased in steady increments after he attended boarding school, entered Oxford, and fought and was injured in World War I.

Becoming a Christian was a gradual process for Lewis. He was inspired in part by writers George MacDonald and G. K. Chesterton. In his book *Surprised by*

Joy, he explained that his friend J. R. R. Tolkien, author of the *Lord of the Rings*, also influenced his spiritual and religious beliefs.

Lewis incorporated many Christian metaphors and biblical references into his popular Narnia series. For example, when Caspian is made King of Narnia, Aslan—who is the Christ figure of the books—tells him, "You come from the Lord Adam and the Lady Eve. And that is both honor enough to erect the head of the poorest beggar, and shame enough to bow the shoulders of the greatest emperor in earth. Be content."

Lewis wrote more than thirty books, among them *Mere Christianity* and *A Grief Observed,* which he wrote after his wife, American writer Joy Davidman, died of cancer not long after they were married. In it, he explores the connection between grief and faith in personal detail.

"You never know how much you really believe anything until its truth or falsehood becomes a matter of life and death to you," he wrote. "It is easy to say you believe a rope to be strong and sound as long as you are merely using it to cord a box. But suppose you had to hang by that rope over a precipice. Wouldn't you then first discover how much you really trusted it?" ■

Top: C.S. Lewis, 26 October 1956, photo by Keystone Pictures USA/ZUMAPRESS
Left: A complete seven-book boxed set of C.S. Lewis' classic Chronicles of Narnia series.

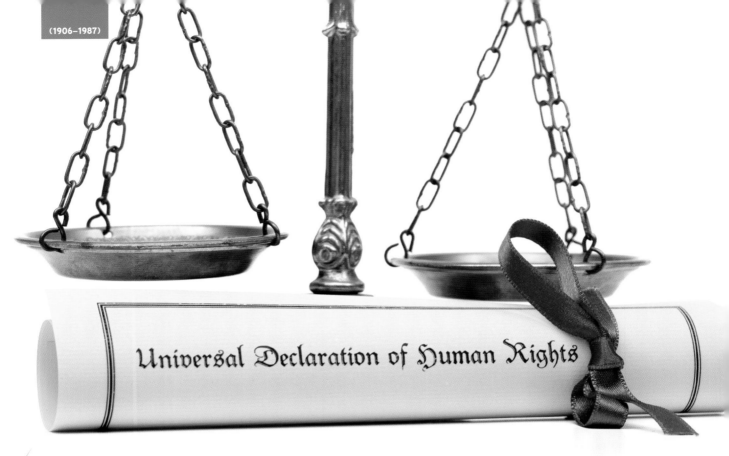

78 Charles Malik

While he enjoyed an impressive forty-year diplomatic and academic career, Charles Malik was most proud of his work as the chief architect of the Universal Declaration of Human Rights (UDHR). Proclaimed by the United Nations General Assembly in Paris on December 10, 1948, the UDHR was a breakthrough for human rights. While the Bible is not directly quoted in the UDHR, the document certainly was influenced by biblical ideas.

Translated into more than 500 languages, the document calls for a common standard for all peoples and nations, among them the right to education; the right to freedom of thought, conscience, and religion; the freedom from "arbitrary arrest, detention, or exile"; and the freedom from "cruel, inhuman, or degrading treatment or punishment."

Born in Lebanon, Charles Malik received his PhD in philosophy from Harvard University and taught there as well as the American University of Beirut. In his role as diplomat, he served as Lebanon's first ambassador to the United States (1953–55) and to the United Nations (1945–55), and he served as president of the United Nations General Assembly (1958–59).

A Greek Orthodox Christian and noted theologian, Malik wrote several commentaries on the Bible and brought a biblical perspective to his international diplomacy. He was respected by evangelical, Catholic, and orthodox leaders alike. From 1967 to 1971, Malik was president of the World Council on Christian Education, and from 1966 to 1972, he was vice president of the United Bible Societies.

He shared his beliefs about the Bible in an address he called "The Two Tasks," which he gave in 1980 at the opening of the Billy Graham Center at Wheaton College: "The Bible is the source of every good thought and impulse I have," Malik declared. "In the Bible God himself, the Creator of everything from nothing, speaks to me and to the world directly, about himself, about ourselves, and about his will for the course of events and for the consummation of history." ■

79 Dietrich Bonhoeffer

What do you imagine when you hear the words double agent? Perhaps you think of someone dressed in a trench coat and carrying a briefcase based on novels and films set during the Cold War. You probably wouldn't think of a pastor.

However, Dietrich Bonhoeffer was not your typical pastor.

Born into a well-educated, aristocratic German family, Bonhoeffer decided at the age of fourteen that he wanted to study theology. After completing his doctorate in 1927, Bonhoeffer served as a pastor of a German-speaking congregation in Spain, and he then spent a year as an exchange student at Union Theological Seminary in New York City. He wrote that he was particularly inspired by the worship at the African American churches he attended in Harlem.

In both locations and then again when he returned to Germany in 1931, Bonhoeffer worked with the poor. Accustomed to helping the downtrodden, he spoke out against anti-Semitism from the time Hitler came to power in 1933. He led the Confessing Church, the Protestant movement that opposed Nazism by declaring that the Bible, not the state, was the supreme authority.

As a member of the German Intelligence Office (the *Abwehr*), Bonhoeffer was supposed to use his contacts to help Adolph Hitler gain information about other countries. In reality, however, he delivered news

to the Allies about Hitler, and he used his authority to smuggle Jews out of Germany in *Operation 7*. In 1940, Bonhoeffer publicly declared his defiance by publishing a book on the Psalms titled *The Prayer Book of the Bible*, which emphasized the Old Testament's importance by implication and used pro-Jewish language throughout.

Bonhoeffer led an underground seminary that was shut down by the Nazis in 1940. He wrote about his experiences in his books *The Cost of Discipleship* and *Life Together*.

As his involvement with *Operation 7* and the German resistance movement became apparent, Bonhoeffer was arrested in 1943. He was sent to prison and then later to a concentration camp. He encouraged other prisoners and prison guards throughout this difficult time, and in his *Letters and Papers from Prison*—published after his death—he wrote about keeping strong in faith while living under harsh circumstances.

He referenced the Bible frequently in his words and his writings. An example is his statement, "When Christ calls a man, he bids him come and die," which parallels Jesus's words from Matthew 16:24–25: "If anyone would come after me, let him deny himself and take up his cross and follow me. For whoever would save his life will lose it, but whoever loses his life for my sake will find it."

Bonhoeffer was executed just one month before Germany surrendered to the Allies, leaving much of his writing incomplete, including a volume on Christian ethics. However, his writings continue to inspire readers today. ∎

Top: Stamp printed by Germany, shows Dietrich Bonhoeffer, circa 1995.
Left: Dietrich Bonhoeffer Memorial in Flossenberg concentration camp **89**

80 Rabbi Abraham Joshua Heschel

Although he was the most noted Jewish theologian of the twentieth century, Abraham Joshua Heschel's influence went far beyond Judaism.

Forced to flee his homeland of Poland due to the Nazi invasion during World War II, Heschel frequently wrote on the theme of justice. He often referenced passages from the Bible to illustrate his points. For example, in his book *The Prophets*, Heschel discussed the balance between divine inspiration and human personality and the biblical prophet's role as a mouthpiece for God. He also emphasized the important social role that Amos, Hosea, Isaiah, Micah, Jeremiah, and Habakkuk served when they unflinchingly spoke the truth to those in power.

Heschel participated in the United States civil rights movement alongside Martin Luther King Jr. After marching with King in Selma, Alabama, he commented, "Legs are not lips, and walking is not kneeling. And yet our legs uttered songs. Even without words, our march was worship. I felt my legs were praying."

Jewish support of the anti-Vietnam War protest movement, the civil rights movement, and the human rights of the Soviet Jewry movement were largely due to Heschel's influence. He also worked with the Catholic Church during Vatican II to help heal the divisions between Christians and Jews.

From 1946 to 1972, while serving at the Jewish Theological Seminary of America as professor of Jewish ethics and mysticism, Heschel published a number of significant works, including *The Sabbath: Its Meaning for Modern Man* (1951), *Man Is Not Alone: A Philosophy of Religion* (1951), and *God in Search of Man* (1955). *The Prophets* (1961), which Heschel originally developed as his doctrinal thesis, is viewed as a masterpiece of biblical scholarship. ∎

Top: Abraham Joshua Heschel - 1970s portrait
Left: Tallit, a Jewish symbol of prayer

Although she was canonized in 2016 as Saint Teresa of Calcutta, the world remembers her as Mother Teresa—an international symbol of charity who devoted her life to helping India's poor and sick.

Seemingly small and even frail in appearance—she stood only five feet tall and was often stooped in her later years—Mother Teresa was amazingly strong in spirit and in purpose.

Pop singer Bob Geldorf, who was in Ethiopia participating in his Band Aid fundraising campaign, witnessed her strength firsthand in 1985. At Addis Ababa Airport, he watched the petite nun boldly confront a government official about two unused buildings she wanted to use as orphanages. The official hesitated but agreed.

"There was a certainty of purpose which left her little patience," Geldorf recalled. "But she was totally selfless; every moment her aim seemed to be, how can I use this or that situation to help others?"

Mother Teresa was born in Macedonia as Anjezë Gonxhe Bojaxhiu. She felt called to a religious life at the age of twelve. At eighteen, she left her home and family to pursue that call, and at nineteen, she was living in Calcutta, training to become a teacher and nun. She spent two decades there, primarily teaching girls at Loreto Covenant. In 1946, however, she received what she described as a second call from God to devote herself to serving the city's poorest and sickest people.

With no supplies or equipment, she often improvised, sometimes using a wooden spoon to write in the dirt to teach children from the slums of Calcutta. In 1950, she founded the Missionaries of Charity, whose members took the traditional vows of obedience, service to the poor, poverty, and chastity. The organization, which grew to include 4,500 sisters in branches in 133 countries, continues its work today. In 1979, Mother Teresa was awarded the Nobel Peace Prize for her efforts.

Mother Teresa was motivated by her faith and trust in God. She often referenced the Bible in her work. She found inspiration in Jesus's words on the cross from John 19:28, "I thirst." She believed Jesus was thirsting for the love of those who did not believe in him. Mother Teresa also often quoted Jesus's words from Matthew 25:40: "And the King shall answer and say unto them, Verily I say unto you, Inasmuch as ye have done it unto one of the least of these my brethren, ye have done it unto me" (KJV). ∎

82 Ronald Reagan

Bringing his skills as a radio broadcaster and an actor to the White House, Ronald Reagan was called "the Great Communicator."

Reagan combined his likable personality with his resolve to restore what he termed "the great, confident roar of American progress and growth and optimism" at home while achieving what he dubbed "peace with strength" abroad. His two terms helped define 1980s America, and his legacy includes helping bring about the end of the Cold War.

He survived an assassination attempt early in his first term, and brought new attention to Alzheimer's disease through his battle with it near the end of his life.

Born in Tampico, Illinois, Ronald Reagan and his family eventually settled in Dixon, Illinois. Reagan was an athlete, student body president, and actor at Dixon High School. He went on to be active in sports and theater at Eureka College and then became a sports radio broadcaster after he graduated in 1932.

While in Los Angeles covering the Chicago Cubs, Reagan did a screen test with Warner Brothers. He signed an acting contract and appeared in more than fifty movies over the next thirty years. His best-known role is as George Gipp in the 1950 film *Knute Rockne, All American,* in which he said, "Win one for the Gipper," a line he often quipped in his political career.

Reagan developed an interest in politics as president of the Screen Actors Guild and as a pro-business public relations representative for General Electric.

Reagan served as governor of California for two terms and then made two unsuccessful bids for the Republican nomination for president before he won it in 1980. He defeated incumbent Jimmy Carter in a landslide and was reelected in another overwhelming decision over Walter Mondale in 1984.

Reagan declared 1983 the Year of the Bible, encouraging "all citizens, each in his or her own way, to reexamine and rediscover its priceless and timeless message." His speeches and writing reveal his reliance on the Bible's principles. For example, in a 1982 letter to football player Greg Brezina, he wrote, "Let me reassure you that 2 Chronicles 7:14 is ever present in my mind. My daily prayer is that God will help me to use this position [as president] to serve Him." Second Chronicles

7:14 states, "If My people who are called by My name will humble themselves, and pray and seek My face, then I will hear from heaven, and will forgive their sin, and will heal their land."

Throughout his presidency, Reagan emphasized Judeo-Christian values, including the inherent dignity of all human beings because they were made in God's image. He often contrasted this belief with the atheistic views of the Soviet Union. "Each of us, each of you, is made in the most enduring, powerful image of Western civilization. We're made in the image of God, the image of God, the Creator. This is our power, and this our freedom. This is our future." ■

Top: President Reagan presents an introduction for the Horatio Alger Association in 1985.

83 Wernher von Braun

A proficient student of languages, Wernher von Braun failed mathematics and physics as a young man. However, a love of astronomy passed down from his mother motivated him not only to master the subjects but to excel in them.

Today, the German scientist is known as "the father of rocket science." He developed the first practical space rockets and launch vehicles that have been instrumental in the exploration of space.

Born in Wirsitz, Germany, von Braun's father was a member of the Weimar Republic Cabinet and a founder of the German Savings Bank. His mother was a musician with a keen interest in astronomy.

A telescope his mother gave him and reading Hermann Oberth's *The Rocket into Interplanetary Space* launched von Braun's interest in science. He went on to earn a doctorate degree in physics from the University of Berlin and led an experimental launch of two liquid-fueled rockets.

However, the scientist objected to rockets being used as weapons. After von Braun and 400 members of his research team surrendered to American forces in 1945, he continued his work on US soil. In 1955, he became a citizen of the United States.

Von Braun played a key role on the team that launched the first American artificial earth satellite, *Explorer I*, in 1958; he also pioneered the development of rocketry for NASA. As director of NASA's Marshall Space Flight Center (1960–70), von Braun produced the *Saturn I* rocket and the *Saturn IB* and *Saturn V* space vehicles for the *Apollo 8* mission. Twenty-seven Americans traveled to the moon in his rockets.

Von Braun looked to the Bible for guidance on how scientific knowledge should be used. He explained, according to one account: "In this age of space flight, when we use the modern tools of science to advance into new regions of human activity, the Bible—this grandiose, stirring history of the gradual revelation and unfolding of the moral law—remains in every way an up-to-date book.

"Our knowledge and use of the laws of nature that enable us to fly to the Moon also enable us to destroy our home planet with the atom bomb. . . . Science itself does not address the question whether we should use the power at our disposal for good or for evil. The guidelines of what we ought to do are furnished in the moral law of God. . . . It is no longer enough that we pray that God may be with us on our side. We must learn to pray that we may be on God's side." ∎

84 Jesse Owens

With his record-breaking performance at the 1936 Olympics in Berlin, American track-and-field star Jesse Owens earned gold medals in four events: 100 meters, long jump, 200 meters, and 4×100-meter relay.

At that time, no track-and-field athlete had won so many gold medals in a single Olympics game. Called "the fastest man alive," Owens did more than set speed records—his triumph became a moral victory for those opposed to Adolph Hitler.

Hitler wanted to use the Olympic Games to showcase European talent and to prove that the "Aryan" race was superior to other races. Owens, an African American, discredited Hitler's theory with his amazing performance.

Overcoming bigotry was not new for Owens. As a student at Ohio State University, he was elected as the first black captain of the university's varsity track team but was not allowed to live on campus with his white teammates. But at the 1935 Big Ten Championships, he outperformed his teammates, setting three world records and then tying a fourth record, all within a span of forty-five minutes!

Owens used his experiences to inspire others and often worked with underprivileged youth. In 1976, President Gerald Ford presented Owens with the Medal of Freedom, the nation's highest civilian honor, and, in 1979, President Jimmy Carter bestowed upon him the Living Legend Award.

In his autobiography, he cited a Bible verse that comforted him during a challenging time:

"Some lines from the Bible which my mother taught me kept running through my mind. She always used to make us memorize a different passage every week, but sometimes she would forget and she would keep teaching us the ones she liked over and over throughout the years. This one was from Corinthians, and it might have been her favorite. . . . When I finally shut my eyes, those lines that my mother taught me echoed back again:

But when that which is perfect is come, then that which is in part shall be done away. When I was a child, I spake as a child, I understood as a child, I thought as a child: but when I became a man, I put away childish things (1 Corinthians 13:10–11, KJV)."

Top: A postage stamp printed in USA showing an image of Jesse Owens, circa 1990.
Bottom: Berlin's Olympia Stadium

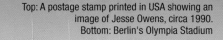

85 Rosa Parks

It started as just a routine bus ride. Tired after a long day's work as a seamstress for a Montgomery, Alabama, department store, Rosa Parks boarded a city bus for the fifteen-minute ride to her apartment on December 1, 1955.

She passed some open seats marked for "Whites Only" for a seat in the middle of the bus that was open to black people. As the bus filled to standing room only, the driver ordered Parks and three other black passengers to give up their seats to white riders.

When Parks politely refused, she was arrested, and she spent the night in the city jail. However, her simple act of noncompliance set off a chain reaction that eventually caused her to be called the "mother of the civil rights movement."

Parks's arrest caught the attention of Martin Luther King Jr., who, along with the Montgomery Improvement Association, led a yearlong boycott against the municipal bus company. Eventually, the segregated seating policy made its way to the US Supreme Court, which declared it unconstitutional on November 13, 1956.

In her autobiography, Parks wrote that the Bible was a constant source of strength in her life.

"In one of the darkest moments of my life . . . I needed help, and I went to Psalms 27:1–7. My mother used to read it to me when I was a child.

The Lord is my light and my salvation; whom shall I fear? The Lord is the strength of my life; of whom shall I be afraid?

When the wicked, even mine enemies and my foes, came upon me to eat up my flesh, they stumbled and fell.

Though an host may encamp against me, my heart shall not fear: though war should rise against me, in this will I be confident. (Psalm 27:1–7, KJV)" ■

Top: Rosa Parks after being arrested for refusal to give up her bus seat in Montgomery, Alabama.

88 Jackie Robinson

Branch Rickey, the president of the Brooklyn Dodgers who recruited Jackie Robinson, had no illusions that life would go smoothly for the first African American player signed to a US professional baseball team.

When Rickey signed Robinson, already a star in Negro league baseball, to a minor league contract in 1945, both men knew Robinson would receive hateful treatment from fans and other players. In fact, Rickey told Robinson he wanted a man who "had guts enough not to fight back."

From then on, Robinson, who made his major league debut on April 15, 1947, showed remarkable restraint. Although he was faced with vicious racial slurs, extreme prejudice, hurled objects, and death threats, Robinson excelled on and off the field as the first African American to play Major League Baseball.

Born in Cairo, Georgia, Jackie Robinson grew up in poverty with his single mother and four older siblings. Robinson's brother Matthew—who won a silver medal in the 200-meter dash at the 1936 Olympic Games in Berlin—inspired Jackie to pursue his incredible talent for athletics. Jackie attended the University of California, Los Angeles, where he became the university's first student to win varsity letters in four sports.

After serving in the United States Army during World War II, Robinson began to play baseball professionally, leading to his eventual deal with Branch Rickey of the Brooklyn Dodgers. In 1947, he was named National League Rookie of the Year, and he earned the Most Valuable Player Award in 1949. In 1955, he led the Dodgers to a World Series win. With a .311 career batting average, he also became the first African American player inducted into the Baseball Hall of Fame. Most significantly, Robinson paved the way for future African American athletes in professional sports.

Both Rickey and Robinson shared a foundation in the Bible. By turning away from vicious racism, Robinson lived out the teachings of Jesus, encouraged by a Bible verse Rickey had shared with him: "But I say unto you, that ye resist not evil: but whosoever shall smite thee on thy right cheek, turn to him the other also" (Matthew 5:39, KJV).

According to his biographer, Arnold Rampersad, Robinson was greatly influenced by his mother, Millie, who took him to church regularly, and by his pastor, Karl Downs, who took him under his wing during Jackie's teenage years and became a father figure to him. Through Rev. Downs's influence, Jackie grew in his faith and even began teaching Sunday school at Scott United Methodist Church in Pasadena, California.

"I had a lot of faith in God," Robinson said when explaining how he dealt with the racism. "There's nothing like faith in God to help a fellow who gets booted around once in a while." ∎

Top: Jackie Robinson street art, 2014 in Montreal, Canada

89 Charles Schulz

Even as a young boy, Charles Schulz wanted to be a cartoonist. But he could never have imagined the far-reaching impact his *Peanuts* characters would have on modern culture.

When Schulz retired in 2000, his cartoon strip about a group of precocious children and an intelligent, lovable dog was syndicated in more than 2,600 newspapers worldwide and was translated in more than twenty-five languages in book collections.

His comic strip impacted the English language with phrases he popularized, such as "security blanket," "Good grief!" "You blockhead," "the true meaning of Christmas," and even "Aaugh!" It also found its way into theme park rides and characters, onto the stage as a hit musical, and as the basis for several beloved holiday TV cartoon programs. NASA even got into the act. In May 1969, the *Apollo 10* crew named their lunar module "Snoopy" and their command module "Charlie Brown."

Yet many people may not realize that the *Peanuts* comic strip broke ground in another way. Nearly 600 *Peanuts* newspaper strips contained a spiritual reference. The references were so relatable that pastors and editors of religious publications frequently requested permission to reprint *Peanuts* strips.

"You can grind out daily gags, but I'm not interested in simply doing gags," Schulz explained. "I'm interested in doing a strip that says something and makes some comment on the important things in life."

Many of his *Peanuts* characters quoted directly from the Bible. For example, in a June 1952 panel, Charlie Brown uses Solomon's phrase from Ecclesiastes 1:14: "All is vanity!" In December 1955, the words of Charlie Brown and Linus to Snoopy are taken from John 16:33: "Be of good cheer, Snoopy . . . Yes, be of good cheer."

In *A Charlie Brown Christmas*, the beloved animated special that has aired every year since it premiered in 1965, the *Peanuts* gang explores the commercialization of Christmas. The character Linus recites directly from the King James Version's Gospel of Luke.

"Little things we say and do in Christ's name are like pebbles thrown into water," said Schulz. "The ripples spread out in circles, and influence people we may know only slightly and sometimes not at all." ∎

Top: Charlie Brown statue in front of Charles Schulz Museum
Right: Charles Schulz (1922-2000), seated at drawing table with drawing of Charlie Brown, 1956

90 Margaret Thatcher

Nicknamed "The Iron Lady" for her strong resolve and fiery speeches, Margaret Thatcher served as the first female prime minister in Britain from 1979 to 1990.

During her controversial time in office, she was both revered and disliked by the British people as she privatized certain industries, reduced trade union powers, lowered public welfare benefits, opposed Soviet communism, and fought a war to maintain British control of the Falkland Islands. She also developed a friendship with President Ronald Reagan that bolstered cooperation between the United States and the United Kingdom.

Due to struggles within her Conservative Party and some of her unpopular decisions, Thatcher was pressured into resigning in 1991 after serving three consecutive terms.

Born in Grantham, England, Thatcher's father ran a grocery store, and her family lived in an apartment above the store. Her father was a member of the town's council, and it was his example that first interested her in politics.

She attended Oxford University to study chemistry and went on to work as a research chemist, which was unusual for a woman at the time. Just two years after graduating from college, Thatcher ran as the conservative candidate for a Dartford parliamentary seat. She lost, but she made a name for herself during the campaign. When she was again selected as a candidate, she won the 1959 election. As a new member of Parliament, Thatcher was determined to reform the Conservative Party. She was elected party leader in 1975, and she won her bid for prime minster in 1979.

In a speech to the Church of Scotland in 1988, Thatcher explained that her political convictions were rooted in her faith. She said she was speaking "personally as a Christian, as well as a politician," and she shared that she saw the Bible as "a view of the universe, a proper attitude to work, and principles to shape economic and social life."

"We must not profess the Christian faith and go to Church simply because we want social reforms and benefits or a better standard of behavior; but because we accept the sanctity of life, the responsibility that comes with freedom and the supreme sacrifice of Christ," she said.

"Any set of social and economic arrangements which is not founded on the acceptance of individual responsibility will do nothing but harm."

Throughout her time as prime minister, Thatcher focused on the individual instead of the state, drawing on the biblical idea of each person being made in the image of God. Like President Ronald Reagan, she frequently contrasted the spiritual and biblical values of the West with the atheism of the Soviet Union, which she said, "commits the *ultimate* infraction of the First Commandment—because it demands the worship of the *state*." ∎

Hon. Margaret Thatcher, British Prime Minister, speaks on July 1, 1991 in London

91 Elie Wiesel

*"**Never shall I forget that night, the first night in camp,** which has turned my life into one long night . . . . Never shall I forget these things, even if I am condemned to live as long as God Himself. Never."*

These haunting words are taken from *Night*, Elie Wiesel's memoir of the Holocaust. Although Wiesel wrote more than fifty books, including other works about the Holocaust, *Messengers of God*, and *Wise Men and Their Tales*, *Night* remains his most important work. Translated into more than thirty languages and with more than seven million copies sold to date, the slim volume has introduced millions of readers to the atrocities of the Holocaust.

Born into a Jewish community in Romania, Wiesel's young life was upended in 1944 when the Nazis invaded his homeland and deported his family to the Auschwitz-Birkenau concentration camp in Poland.

His mother and younger sister were killed, and he was separated from his older sisters. Wiesel and his father managed to stay together, working as slave laborers at the camp. However, they were transferred to Buchenwald, where his father died in January 1945, just three months before Allied troops freed the prisoners.

Wiesel rejoined his older sisters in France when he was sent to an orphanage there. After about ten years, Wiesel became determined not to remain silent about the suffering he endured, so he began to write about his experiences.

In his Nobel Lecture, after he had won the Nobel Peace Prize in 1986, Wiesel referenced the biblical account of Job: "Let us remember Job who, having lost everything—his children, his friends, his possessions, and even his argument with God—still found the strength to begin again, to rebuild his life."

Wiesel continued, "Job was determined not to repudiate the creation, however imperfect, that God had entrusted to him. Job, our ancestor. Job, our contemporary. His ordeal concerns all humanity. Did he ever lose his faith? If so, he rediscovered it within his rebellion. He demonstrated that faith is essential to rebellion, and that hope is possible beyond despair. The source of his hope was memory, as it must be ours. Because I remember, I despair. Because I remember, I have the duty to reject despair. I remember the killers, I remember the victims, even as I struggle to invent a thousand and one reasons to hope." ■

Top: Elie Wiesel attends Lenox Hill hospital fundraising event in New York City for Hurricane Sandy victims
Bottom: Wiesel was awarded the Nobel Peace Prize in 1986.

92 Desmond Tutu

Archbishop Desmond Tutu is best known for his role in helping end apartheid in South Africa, his native country. "The universe can take quite a while to deliver," Tutu once said of the long racial struggle in his country. "God is patient with us to become the God's children he wants us to be, but you really can see him weeping."

Born in Klerksdorp, Tutu grew up in a strictly segregated South Africa. He began his career as an English and history teacher, but he left teaching because of the low standards and funding for black students.

He then enrolled at Saint Peter's Theological College, where he studied the Bible and began the journey toward priesthood. In 1975, Tutu gained national and even international attention when he was named the first black Anglican dean of Johannesburg's Saint Mary's Cathedral. He also served as bishop of Lesotho from 1976 to 1978.

At a time when many anti-apartheid leaders were in prison or exile, Tutu became a prominent spokesman for the movement. He continued to break racial barriers as the first black general secretary of the South African Council of Churches (1978), bishop of Johannesburg (1985), and the first black archbishop of Cape Town (1986). He earned the Nobel Peace Prize in 1984 for his role in opposing apartheid. And in 1995, South African president Nelson Mandela selected him to chair the Truth and Reconciliation Commission Mandela had formed in the aftermath of apartheid.

Tutu is often called South Africa's moral conscience. He has relied on the biblical principles of justice, love, and forgiveness to guide South Africa from apartheid to a modern democracy. Teaching and preaching the Christian message, he has worked to create a South Africa that is "more open and just; where people count and where they have equal access to the good things of life; with equal opportunity to live, work and learn."

He frequently cites 1 Corinthians 6:19 as the foundation for his belief that God created all people to be treated with respect and dignity: He has cited the Exodus story to emphasize his belief that God will deliver people out of slavery and oppression and that people have a responsibility to be part of that deliverance:

'Do you remember what God told Moses? He said "I have seen the suffering of My people, I have heard their cry. I know their suffering and am come down to deliver them.' Our God is a God who knows. Our God is a God who sees. Our God is a God who hears. Our God is a God who comes down to deliver. But the way God delivers us is by using us as His partners, by calling on Moses, and on you and me." ∎

Left: Desmond Tutu at the 2008 Freedom Awards. University of Southern California, Los Angeles, CA. 09-15-08

93 Elvis Presley

Elvis Presley, often referred to as "the King," is undisputedly rock-'n'-roll's first major superstar.

By combining his Southern roots of gospel and country music with blues and jazz—along with his own good looks, vigor, and personality—Presley became an international sensation as a teen idol, movie star, and musical icon.

With estimated sales of more than one billion records internationally, Presley recorded 108 hit songs, with seven of those hitting the number one slot, according to *Billboard* magazine.

Presley, whose twin brother was stillborn, grew up as an only child in East Tupelo, Mississippi. His father had irregular employment as a truck driver, and his family, who attended the First Assembly of God Church, was often in financial straits.

For Presley, superstardom came with trouble and personal tragedy, but he apparently turned to his faith in his difficult times. His King James Version Bible includes many handwritten notes and underlined passages. He seemed to be especially fond of the Psalms, including Psalm 43:3, Psalm 138, Psalm 81:1, and Psalm 149. Of

particular interest is the phrase he wrote in his Bible below Psalm 11: "In the Lord I place my trust and He will guide me."

Presley began his career singing gospel music, and his three Grammy Awards were for gospel albums. One of his most famous gospel songs is "He Touched Me" by Bill Gaither, which describes being changed by Jesus. His song "I, John" refers to the book of Revelation and its traditional author, John, who described seeing heaven, angels, and God's throne. The lyrics include biblical phrases such as "three gates in the east/west/north/south," "twelve gates to the city," "[the man] held twelve bright stars in his right hand / Well his eyes flashed fire like the burning sun."

Presley didn't just enjoy singing biblical lyrics; he also enjoyed discussing the Bible, according to his cousin, Patsy Presley. In fact, it was his custom to carry his Bible with him. According to author Heart Lanier Shapr, some of his favorite scriptures included 1 Corinthians 13, Matthew 6:21, Romans 1:16, and Romans 8. ■

Top: Elvis collectors' memorabilia from the "King of Rock and Roll"
Left: Statue of a young Elvis Presley on Beale Street, Memphis, TN

94 Pope Francis

From the moment Pope Francis assumed his role as head of the Roman Catholic Church on March 13, 2013, it was clear he would be a very different pontiff.

Born Jorge Mario Bergoglio in Buenos Aires, Pope Francis, at age seventy-six, was not only the first Jesuit priest and the first person from the Americas to become pope, but his demeanor and actions quickly established him as "the people's pope."

Francis opted to live in a simple two-room apartment rather than the lavishly appointed papal quarters in the Vatican Apostolic Palace and to ride in an ordinary car—not the flashy "Popemobile." In his first public appearance, he wore the plain, white cassock with an iron pectoral cross instead of the red mozzetta and gold cross.

Pope Francis worked for a short time as a chemical technician and as a nightclub bouncer before he began his seminary studies. In 1969, he was ordained as a priest, and he served as head of the Society of Jesus (Jesuits) in Argentina from 1973 to 1979.

In 1998, he was named archbishop of Buenos Aires, and Pope John Paul II appointed him as cardinal in 2001. When Pope Benedict XVI resigned in 2013, a papal conclave named Jorge Bergoglio as his successor.

Pope Francis demonstrates a concern for helping the poor and for bringing together people of different backgrounds. He was nominated for the Nobel Peace Prize and was named *Time* magazine's 2013 Man of the Year.

Pope Francis, in an interview published in *America* magazine in 2013, mentioned several Bible passages that helped shape his views on humility and compassion. He quoted his motto, "Miserando atque Eligendo" [By Having Mercy and by Choosing Him], which references Matthew, the despised tax collector Jesus called to follow him (Matthew 9:9).

He also referred to Jesus's parable of the good Samaritan (Luke 10:25–37), explaining, "The thing the church needs most today is the ability to heal wounds and to warm the hearts of the faithful; it needs nearness, proximity. I see the church as a field hospital after battle. . . . The church's ministers must be merciful, take responsibility for the people and accompany them like the good Samaritan, who washes, cleans and raises up his neighbor." ■

Pope Francis greets the pilgrims during his weekly general audience in St. Peter's square at the Vatican on April 9, 2014

95 Bob Marley

Jamaican singer-songwriter Bob Marley introduced the rhythm, energy, and soulful sounds of reggae to the world. With sales of more than 75 million records, his popularity and influence continue today.

"The real secret is that Marley's music is about something," wrote Roger Steffens in a 2000 article for *The Beat* magazine. "It has value. Bob's art is life transforming, answering our highest needs."

Born in Jamaica, Marley grew up in poverty. In his youth, he looked to music for solace. He enjoyed listening to American artists such as Ray Charles, Fats Domino, Elvis Presley, and the Drifters on the radio. In his compositions, he combined those influential styles with the Ska and Rocksteady musical genres popular in Jamaica to create a new sound. Some of his best-known songs are "Adam and Eve," "No Woman, No Cry," "Three Little Birds," "Buffalo Soldier," "Redemption Song," and "One Love/People Get Ready."

One scholar identified 137 biblical themes, allusions, and metaphors in Marley's songs. With his lyrics, Marley revealed that he respected the Bible and turned to it often to learn about life. Marley biographer Stephen Davis stated, "Bob would often consult and quote from the weathered Bible he carried with him." Mick Carter, one of Marley's tour promoters, commented that while on tour, "The Bibles would come out and the arguments would become very heated."

Marley's 1973 song "Stiff-Necked Fools," an anthem against vanity and materialism, is an example of how the Bible influenced Marley's music. Its title and lyrics originate from numerous biblical passages, such as Exodus 33:3–5; Proverbs 10:15, 21 and 18:11; and Romans 1:21.

His "We and Dem" refers to justice for the shedding of innocent blood (a theme in many biblical books) and includes the phrase, "It's what the Bible say, yeah! yeah!" His "Babylon System" references "trodding on the winepress" from Job, Isaiah, and Revelation, and his song "Survival" compares contemporary victims of violence to Shadrach, Meshach, and Abednego from Daniel 6.

Marley's final song on his last album, "Redemption," which he completed before he succumbed to cancer at the age of thirty-six, urges listeners to follow the teachings of the Bible with the lyric "We've got to fulfill the book." ■

Bob Marley abstract graffiti in the Green Light District in Copenhagen

96 Francis Collins

In a culture that often refers to genetic scientists as "playing God," Francis Collins stands out as someone who sees no conflict between science and creation. In fact, he embraces both.

As the director of the Human Genome Project, Francis Collins, MD, PhD, led a group of scientists as they read and deciphered the 3.1 billion units that comprise the DNA blueprint for human beings.

After beginning his career as an assistant professor at the University of Michigan at Ann Arbor, Collins earned a reputation as one of the world's leading genetics researchers. He led studies to discover the genes that cause cystic fibrosis, neurofibromatosis, and Huntington chorea.

In 1993, Collins left the University of Michigan to lead the National Center for Human Genome Research, which was working on the Human Genome Project, a $3 billion effort coordinating multiple academic research centers. Collins was nominated as head of the National Institutes of Health by President Barack Obama in 2009 and again in 2017 by President Donald Trump.

In 2000, a White House press conference announced the assembly of a working draft of the human genome was complete. The mapping of the human genome was lauded as a first step toward helping doctors diagnose and treat diseases caused by genetic disorders.

As a scientist and someone who reads the Bible, Collins addresses the topic of creation. "Yes, evolution by descent from a common ancestor is clearly true," he states. "If there was any lingering doubt about the evidence from the fossil record, the study of DNA provides the strongest possible proof of our relatedness to all other living things."

"But why couldn't this be God's plan for creation?" he asks. "True, this is incompatible with an ultra-literal interpretation of Genesis, but long before Darwin, there were many thoughtful interpreters like Saint Augustine, who found it impossible to be exactly sure what the meaning of that amazing creation story was supposed to be. So, attaching oneself to such literal interpretations in the face of compelling scientific evidence pointing to the ancient age of Earth and the relatedness of living things by evolution seems neither wise nor necessary for the believer."

"I have found there is a wonderful harmony in the complementary truths of science and faith," stated Collins in a 2007 article he wrote for CNN. "The God of the Bible is also the God of the genome. God can be found in the cathedral or in the laboratory. By investigating God's majestic and awesome creation, science can actually be a means of worship." ∎

Top: Dr. Francis Collins, former director of the Human Genome Project, Now Director of the National Institutes of Health

97 Bono

His name is Paul D. Hewson, but the world knows him simply as Bono. When he was in high school in Dublin, Ireland, he was nicknamed "Bono Vox," a loose Latin translation of "good voice," and a shortened version stuck with him.

Bono is the lead singer and main songwriter of the Irish band U2, but he is almost as well known for his international humanitarian efforts as for his musical career. *Time* magazine named him a "Person of the Year" in 2005, and Queen Elizabeth II knighted him in 2007. He has been nominated three times for the Nobel Peace Prize, and Chile awarded him the Pablo Neruda International Presidential Medal of Honor in 2004.

The son of a Roman Catholic postal worker and a Protestant mother, who died when he was fourteen, Bono and U2 achieved some musical success early, but it was the band's fifth studio album *The Joshua Tree* that made them stars.

Bono frequently uses religious, social, and political themes in his songs. He often references the Bible's book of Psalms. For example, his lyrics for the song "40" directly corresponds to Psalm 40. Bono wrote that he appreciates this psalm for "its suggestion that in time, grace will replace karma and love replace the very strict law of Moses."

In the introduction that he wrote for *Selections from the Book of Psalms,* published by Canongate Books in 1999, Bono explains that the Psalms introduced him to God and "led [him] to the poetry of Ecclesiastes, the Song of Solomon, the book of John." He once said that he sees David as the "Elvis of the Bible" and that he believes the Psalms are the original blues music.

In 2016, Fuller studio produced a short film with Bono and Eugene Peterson, author of *The Message* Bible, to encourage people to read the psalms. While on tour in 2001, the singer often quoted lines from Peterson's interpretation of Psalm 116 as an introduction to the U2 hit "Where the Streets Have No Name." ■

Bono of band "U2" in the Willy Brandt House of the SPD, Berlin.

98 Barack Obama

Raised in Hawaii and Indonesia by his single mother and his grandparents, Barak Obama became the first African American to serve as president of the United States. His story is a modern American success story.

Obama's father, Barack Obama Sr., grew up herding goats in Kenya. Later, he earned a scholarship to study at the University of Hawaii. It was there he met and married Ann Dunham, Obama's mother. Obama's parents divorced when he was a toddler.

Obama excelled in school in Hawaii, and he studied at Occidental College in Los Angeles for two years before transferring to Columbia University and graduating with a degree in political science in 1983. In 1985, he moved to Chicago, where he worked as a community organizer for low-income South Side residents. It was during this time that Obama—who went on to study law at Harvard University and to become a US senator for Illinois—joined the Trinity United Church of Christ.

Although he was not raised in a religious household, Obama admitted that as an adult he turns to the Bible for strength, encouragement, and wisdom. He cited Psalm 46 as a favorite passage. He also stated that during difficult times, he leans on Isaiah 40:31: "But those who hope in the Lord will renew their strength. They will soar on wings like eagles; they will run and not grow weary, they will walk and not be faint."

As a two-term president, Obama made Bible study and prayer part of his daily routine. He appointed Joshua DuBois as his "Pastor-in-Chief," and DuBois sent Obama daily inspirational devotionals. Obama often invited pastors to the White House to pray with him for wisdom and strength. He also contacted DuBois regularly to help him choose an appropriate quote from the Bible to comfort or challenge the nation.

President Obama often quoted the Bible in significant speeches, in the wake of tragedy or triumph. In a televised address on November 20, 2014, President Obama used Exodus 23:9 to promote his immigration program to the American people. The biblical text says, "You shall not oppress a sojourner. You know the heart of a sojourner, for you were sojourners in the land of Egypt." In his speech, Obama echoed the words of the Bible: "Scripture tells us that we shall not oppress a stranger, for we know the heart of a stranger— we were strangers once, too. My fellow Americans, we are and always will be a nation of immigrants. We were strangers once, too." ■

US Senator Barack Obama speaking at Change We Need Presidential rally, at Verizon Wireless Virginia Beach Amphitheater on October 30, 2008

99 J. K. Rowling

With its core theme as the classic battle between good and evil, the Harry Potter franchise—which includes books, films, a theme park, and merchandise—is estimated to be worth about $25 billion. *Time* magazine estimates the wealth of the woman behind the franchise, author J. K. Rowling, at more than $1.2 billion.

Living in Edinburgh, Scotland as a single mother, Joanne Rowling was struggling to make ends meet when she wrote the first Harry Potter novel under the pen name J. K. Rowling, using her grandmother's name, Kathleen, for the second initial. That first book and its sequels follow the life of a young wizard, his friends, his teachers, and his enemies at Hogwarts School of Witchcraft and Wizardry.

After numerous rejections, Rowling sold the first book, *Harry Potter and the Sorcerer's Stone*, for about $4,000. While the first book, published in 1997, was a huge success—especially for a book aimed at young readers—it was only the beginning. Each new Harry Potter book had numerous preorders and long lines of eager readers. Today, the Harry Potter books have been translated into more than 60 languages and have sold more than 400 million copies worldwide.

Although some religious leaders denounced the books because of their sorcery-related content, the books contain numerous biblical references and themes. "To me [the religious parallels have] always been obvious," Rowling said in a press conference in 2007. "But I never wanted to talk too openly about it because I

thought it might show people who just wanted the story where we were going."

J.K. Rowling was raised in an Anglican tradition, but not in a religious household. "I was very drawn to faith," she recalled. "I certainly had this need for something that I wasn't getting at home, so I was the one who went out looking for religion."

In the final book of the series, *Harry Potter and the Deathly Hallows*, Harry finds two biblical quotes on tombstones. He sees the Bible verse "The last enemy that shall be destroyed is death" (1 Corinthians 15:26, KJV) at the grave of his loved ones. The tombstones of Albus Dumbledore's mother and sister are etched with the words of Matthew 6:21: "Where your treasure is, there will your heart be also" (KJV).

"I think those two particular quotations he finds on the tombstones . . . they sum up, they almost epitomize the whole series," Rowling said regarding her quotations from the Bible. ∎

Top: J.K. Rowling attends the premiere of *Fantastic Beasts and Where To Find Them* at Alice Tully Hall on November 10, 2016, in New York City
Left: J.K. Rowling's Harry Potter books in a shop in Windsor, England

ART CREDITS

• **page 1** Tim Graham/Alamy Stock Photo • **page 6** Roman Yanushevsky/Shutterstock.com • **page 7** Commons Wikimedia • **page 8** Natalia Paklina/Shutterstock.com; Bill Perry/Shutterstock.com • **page 9** PRISMA ARCHIVO/Alamy Stock Photo • **page 10** Anatoly Maslennikov/Shutterstock.com; Pictorial Press Ltd/Alamy Stock Photo • **page 11** Lebrecht Music and Arts Photo Library/Alamy Stock Photo; Phant/Shutterstock.com • **page 12** Classic Image/Alamy Stock Photo • **page 13** FXQuadro/Shutterstock.com; Classic Image/Alamy Stock Photo • **page 14** Millionstock/Shutterstock.com; INTERFOTO/Alamy Stock Photo • **page 15** GL Archive/Alamy Stock Photo; Lefteris Papaulakis/Shutterstock.com • **page 16** Zvonimir Atletic/Shutterstock.com; Catarina Belova/Shutterstock.com • **page 17** Sibrikov Valery/Shutterstock.com; North Wind Picture Archives/Alamy Stock Photo • **page 18** Jan Schneckenhaus/Shutterstock.com; Morphart Creation/Shutterstock.com • **page 19** Brandon Bourdages/Shutterstock.com; Theera Disayarat/Shutterstock.com • **page 20** Leo Blanchette/Shutterstock.com; Everett Historical/Shutterstock.com • **page 21** Oleg Golovnev/Shutterstock.com • **page 22** pryzmat/Shutterstock.com; dmitry_islentev/Shutterstock.com • **page 23** PRISMA ARCHIVO/Alamy Stock Photo; Sergey Kohl/Shutterstock.corn • **page 24** Alexandra Reinwald/Shutterstock.com; PRISMA ARCHIVO/Alamy Stock Photo • **page 25** PRISMA ARCHIVO/Alamy Stock Photo; Marc Bruxelle/Shutterstock.com • **page 26** Nathan Holland/Shutterstock.com; Classic Image/Alamy Stock Photo • **page 27** RossHelen/Shutterstock.com; North Wind Picture Archives/Alamy Stock Photo • **page 28** Hwa Cho Yi/Shutterstock.com; World History Archive/Alamy Stock Photo • **page 29** Philip Lange/Shutterstock.com; Bill Perry/Shutterstock.com • **page 30** Vadim Sadovski/Shutterstock.com; Elena Korn/Shutterstock.com • **page 31** Heritage Image Partnership Ltd/Alamy Stock Photo • **page 32** vvoronov/Shutterstock.com; Claudio Divizia/Shutterstock.com • **page 33** Glasshouse Images/Alamy Stock Photo; Shelly Still/Shutterstock.com • **page 34** Anna Kucherova/Shutterstock.com; Art Collection 3/Alamy Stock Photo • **page 35** Lebrecht Music and Arts Photo Library/Alamy Stock Photo • **page 36** Niday Picture Library/Alamy Stock Photo; shippee/Shutterstock.com • **page 37** Everett - Art/Shutterstock.com; Julia Sanders/Shutterstock.com • **page 38** Everett Historical/Shutterstock.com; DmitryCh/Shutterstock.com • **page 39** Robert B. Miller/Shutterstock.com; Classic Image/Alamy Stock Photo • **page 40** Georgios Kollidas/Shutterstock.com; Todd Taulman Photography/Shutterstock.com • **page 41** Everett Historical/Shutterstock.com; Wi Holy/Shutterstock.com • **page 42** Kodda/Shutterstock.com; FineArt/Alamy Stock Photo • **page 43** World History Archive/Alamy Stock Photo • **page 44** Everett - Art/Shutterstock.com; auhaus1000/iStock photo • **page 45** Fer Gregory/Shutterstock.com • **page 46** GL Archive/Alamy Stock Photo; Verlena Van Adel/Shutterstock.com • **page 47** Chronicle/Alamy Stock Photo; 19th era/Alamy Stock Photo • **page 48** ra3rn/Shutterstock.com • **page 49** Everett Historical/Shutterstock.com; Daniel M. Silva/Shutterstock.com • **page 50** Everett Historical/Shutterstock.com • **page 51** Everett - Art/Shutterstock.com; Joseph Sohm/Shutterstock.com • **page 52** Everett - Art/Shutterstock.com; Billion Photos/Shutterstock.com • **page 53** /Alamy Stock Photo; canadastock/Shutterstock.com; Everett Historical/Shutterstock.com • **page 54** Everett Collection Historical/Alamy Stock Photo; Art Directors & TRIP/Alamy Stock Photo • **page 55** Everett Historical/Shutterstock.com; Lebrecht Music and Arts Photo Library/Alamy Stock Photo • **page 56** traveler1116/istockphoto.com; Lebrecht Music and Arts Photo Library/Alamy Stock Photo • **page 57** Paul Fearn/Alamy Stock Photo; Old Paper Studios/Alamy Stock Photo • **page 58** GL Archive/Alamy Stock Photo • **page 59** Everett Historical/Shutterstock.com • **page 60** Everett Historical/Shutterstock.com; CBW/Alamy Stock Photo • **page 61** Everett Historical/Shutterstock.com; Ben Molyneux/Alamy Stock Photo • **page 62** Everett Historical/Shutterstock.com; Everett Historical/Shutterstock.com • **page 63** Everett Historical/Shutterstock.com; Morphart Creation/Shutterstock.com • **page 64** Everett Historical/Shutterstock.com; Paul Fearn/Alamy Stock Photo; Everett Historical/Shutterstock.com; Everett Historical/Shutterstock.com • **page 66** Heidi Besen/Shutterstock.com • **page 67** Paul Fearn/Alamy Stock Photo • **page 68** IgorGolovniov/Shutterstock.com • **page 69** Commons Wikimedia; ZU_09/istockphoto.com • **page 70** Commons Wikimedia • **page 71** Sean Pavone/Alamy Stock Photo; Commons Wikimedia • **page 72** Everett Historical/Shutterstock.com; Susan Law Cain/Shutterstock.com • **page 73** Commons Wikimedia; tomertu/Shutterstock.com • **page 74** tviolet/Shutterstock.com • **page 76** isidro Lopez/Shutterstock.com; Olga Popova/Shutterstock.com • **page 77** Vladimir Wrangel/Shutterstock.com • **page 78** Georgios Kollidas/Shutterstock.com; MarkoV87/Shutterstock.com • **page 79** Photo 12/Alamy Stock Photo; shalunts/istockphoto.com • **page 80** mike mckavett/Alamy Stock Photo; Dan Josephson/Shutterstock.com; Georgios Kollidas/Shutterstock.com • **page 81** Hemis/Alamy Stock Photo • **page 82** Daniel M. Silva/Shutterstock.com • **page 83** ITAR-TASS Photo Agency/Alamy Stock Photo; Alpha Historica/Alamy Stock Photo • **page 84** mike mckavett/Alamy Stock Photo; Nok Lek/Shutterstock.com; INTERFOTO/Alamy Stock Photo • **page 85** Pictorial Press Ltd/Alamy Stock Photo; M DOGAN/Shutterstock.com • **page 86** Commons Wikimedia • **page 87** Keystone Pictures USA/Alamy Stock Photo; ideabug/istockphoto.com • **page 88** corgarashu/Shutterstock.com • **page 89** rook76/Shutterstock.com; SLashuk/Shutterstock.com • **page 90** Everett Collection Inc/Alamy Stock Photo; MstudioG/Shutterstock.com • **page 91** Clara/Shutterstock.com • **page 92** Joseph Sohm/Shutterstock.com • **page 93** RGB Ventures/SuperStock/Alamy Stock Photo • **page 94** meunierd/Shutterstock.com; catwalker/Shutterstock.com; meunierd/Shutterstock.com • **page 95** Science History Images/Alamy Stock Photo • **page 96** Evdoha_spb/Shutterstock.com • **page 97** Anthony Correia/Shutterstock.com • **page 98** Adam Vilimek/Shutterstock.com; meunierd/Shutterstock.com • **page 99** Stan DaMan/Shutterstock.com; Everett Collection Inc/Alamy Stock Photo • **page 100** David Fowler/Shutterstock.com; David Fowler/Shutterstock.com • **page 101** lev radin/Shutterstock.com; Ryan Rodrick Beiler/Shutterstock.com • **page 102** s_bukley/Shutterstock.com • **page 103** Dan Kosmayer/Shutterstock.com; Joseph Sohm/Shutterstock.com • **page 104** giulio napolitano/Shutterstock.com • **page 106** Lucian Milasan/Shutterstock.com • **page 107** Michael Ventura/Alamy Stock Photo • **page 108** 360b/Shutterstock.com • **page 109** Joseph Sohm/Shutterstock.com; Joseph Sohm/Shutterstock.com • **page 110** JStone/Shutterstock.com; Anton_Ivanov/Shutterstock.com

museum of the Bible

Experience the Book that Shapes History

Museum of the Bible is a 430,000-square-foot building located in the heart of Washington, D.C.—just steps from the National Mall and the U.S. Capitol. Displaying artifacts from several collections, the Museum explores the Bible's history, narrative and impact through high-tech exhibits, immersive settings, and interactive experiences. Upon entering, you pass through two massive, bronze gates resembling printing plates from Genesis 1. Beyond the gates, an incredible replica of an ancient artifact containing Psalm 19 hangs behind etched glass panels. Come be inspired by the imagination and innovation used to display thousands of years of biblical history.

Museum of the Bible aims to be the most technologically advanced museum in the world, starting with its unique Digital Guide that allows guests to personalize their museum experience with navigation, customized tours, supplemental visual and audio content, and more.

**For more information and to plan your visit, go to
museumoftheBible.org.**

Complete Your Collection

To find more books in this series, visit: MuseumoftheBibleBooks.com